Thanks to anyone and everyone I've ever worked
with in this business.

Good or bad, living or dead, you all taught me
everything that I know.

Also... thank you Bob & Nancy for everything else.

INTRODUCTION

This is a book about empathy. If you decide not to read the rest of these words, you must only remember one thing. The secret of excellent restaurant work is universal empathy.

Ta-da.

The hard thing is the "universal" part — that's empathy for everyone — even the assholes. Full disclosure: I have despised many people over the years. People are fucking terrible. I'm a person, I should know.

That said, after empathy, the next most important skill is knowing how to respond to things. This book attempts to break down how to make both quality short term and long term decisions in a restaurant environment.

Lastly, the third skill one needs to master is how to negotiate negatives into positives.

Whew.

Now that that's out of the way. I love working in restaurants. It's challenging, the people are great, and it's deeply rewarding.

It's also not for everyone.

I think of this as a book for the beginner, but it's not comprehensive. I also hope there's something in here for everyone, even the more seasoned worker. I think of this as a guide toward better information.

There's stuff in here that you'll disagree with and stuff that will make you roll your eyes. A lot of this is my opinion, and not every opinion is valid. These are ways of thinking developed over years of working in restaurants. I reference some science, but I am not a scientist. I probably got some of it wrong. There are also exercises here that may or may not help you.

The real value here is in discussing some of these ideas amongst your coworkers. Hash it out.

The only thing you have total control over is yourself, yet, restaurants are a team sport. The job is so much better when you're all on the same page.

What follows may be total horse-shit. But, as long as you're working with a team that agrees on what is horse-shit — you'll all be okay. Pre-shift over.

On with the horse-shit.

THE ART OF GIVING A FUCK

"What is it in me that continues to drive me. It's desire. Desire. Desire trumps passion every time. It's nice to be passionate, and passion is going help move that desire higher. But when that passion's not there, what do you need? That desire. That strong sense of desire."

- THOMAS KELLER, NOVEMBER 11, 2010, TEDX, "THE REACH OF THE RESTAURANT"

"I can teach anybody anything, except I can't teach anyone to give a fuck."

- UNKNOWN RESTAURANT MANAGER

You can barely pass a knife's blade between a decent server and great server.

Lousy service is easy to identify. It leaves people feeling angry, anxious, and frustrated. At its worst, it leaves someone hungry. Cleanliness, attentiveness, and respect go without saying. If you don't already know this, what I'm writing here won't help.

We'll cover some nuts and bolts, but that stuff is easy. The hard thing is to give a fuck.

The simple fact is that if you want to be great at waiting tables, you are an anomaly. It's difficult to give a fuck about waiting because it's a job with no intrinsic glamour. That shouldn't be the case. Done well, the job is challenging and can teach you a great deal.

Plus, restaurants are currently *the* American industry.

The following comes from an August 2017 article by Derek Thompson ("Restaurants Are the New Factories") from *The Atlantic*:

> *"Restaurant jobs are on fire in 2017, growing faster than health care, construction, or manufacturing. The Bureau of Labor Statistics calls this subsector 'food services and drinking places,' and the jobs are mostly at sit-down restaurants, which make up 50 percent of the category. Fast-food joints are the next-largest employer in the category, with 37 percent."*

This means is that this is a big area to explore and there's a lot of opportunities.

But the opportunity is only there if you give a fuck.

Working as a server is a stop-gap kind of job. It's a handy way to take a step towards something else. Some people become servers because it's the next step up in the restaurant hierarchy. Sometimes they're waiting for a different job. Serving feels temporary. Artists, college students, or people trying to get back on their feet fill the position. It has flexible hours. It can offer fast cash. You don't need special education to get started. It's a business that's always hiring.

This is a disposable job.

I recently saw a chart that claimed the average tenure for any restaurant job was one month and twenty-six days.[1] Out of all restaurant jobs, three were significantly above that average. Bartender. Chef. Manager.

My theory is that these are the three positions that give you some form of respect.

The other positions (cook, dishwasher, host, busser, and server) are "bare minimum" employment. A server is the best of the bunch with an average tenure of a month and twenty-seven days. I think it ranks higher because much of the time it's the job that brings in the most money. Still, the Bureau of Labor Statistics reports that, on average, all these positions fall amongst the ten lowest paid jobs in the country.

People have a low perception of all these positions.

Low regard, coupled with high turnover, results in a glut of bad to mediocre servers. Most of us have succumbed to a bad server at some point. There are so many out there that a lot of people seem to prepare for bad service. It's accepted as a reality, and the cycle of mediocrity continues.

Popular wisdom states that everyone should wait tables at some point.

This is bullshit.

If people use something with regularity, (be it gun, car, or blender), they should understand how it works. Because of that, I believe that everyone who uses a restaurant should know how a restaurant works. But no, not everyone should be a server. Bad servers make it harder for everyone else.

This is a job that will provide you with a basic understanding of psychology, sales, culture, food, and more. But only if you pay attention.

"But," I hear you asking, "isn't there a popular philosophy about NOT giving a fuck? If this is just a temporary job, how many fucks should I be giving?" That point of view is about fearing judgment from others and not being yourself. I'm talking about caring about what you do. A fuck's value is in where you put it.

You will need to figure out your own motivations, but here's why I give a fuck.

I'm mainstream. I had a stable and unremarkable upbringing. I'm a white guy from the United States with an ex-girlfriend who once complained that I was, "too heteronormative."

I don't even qualify as vanilla. I am "sweet cream."

Even with that, I never felt comfortable in my skin until I started working in restaurants.

Restaurants were a collection of wild and disparate people. New (to me) cultures, food and beer nerds, angry chefs, happy cooks, soldiers, artists, ex-cons, future cons, and total wack-a-doos. The combination of it all lit up every pleasure center in my brain. Waiting was also a perfect excuse to people watch, talk to strangers, and make new friends.

It wasn't immediate, but eventually, I also became interested in food. That was its own kind of magic. Cooking involves taking raw elements and transforming them into one of a kind events. It's art that literally sustains the person appreciating it. Cooking a meal is sharing a story that gets digested and then becomes a physical part of another person.

Freaky, no?

I left the business. I worked in other fields. But at some point, I realized that restaurants taught me my most valuable skills. It also offered me the opportunity to keep learning. Restaurants showed me how to deal with pressure, problem-solving, and prioritizing. Restaurants taught me how to talk to people, understand them, and how to work with them.

The more I understood how complicated restaurants were, the more I saw a beauty I didn't notice before.

By this point, I'd worked in both terrible places and amazing places. There were valuable lessons in it all. I saw patterns I'd never noticed before. It was like learning another language. One day I woke up and I could "speak restaurant." I started writing on windows, solving Rubik's cubes, and I played chess with strangers in the park. I had become a restaurant genius.

Well, genius is a stretch, but I did start to give a fuck.

Working in a restaurant is hard, complicated, and more than a little nonsensical. It also might *not* get you respect. But, if you can enjoy its challenges, then you should work in a restaurant.

Well, sometimes it *can* get you respect. But what gets you respect is the same thing that makes you good at the job.

Empathy.

Empathy comes out of the moment and is generally defined as caring for others and desiring to help them. To experience real empathy, you must understand what someone needs or wants. It means paying attention, communicating, and identifying causes of discomfort or pain.

For example, someone is gulping water. Why? Is the person hot? Is the food is too salty? Are they nervous and on a first date?

Step one: refill the water.

But it's not only about refilling the water. That's the bare minimum for good service. What is the customer experiencing? If the guest is sweating and fanning themselves, they're probably hot. Offer to reseat them. Give them extra ice. Be a hospitality doctor and diagnose the problem. It's this part that makes for exceptional service.

Here are two solid examples from my life:

I was in a bar with my parents somewhere in Washington state. A mere child, I was a three-foot asshole. A bartender there took the time to show me how to "high five." The guy recognized that I was a child who wanted attention in a place that did not cater to children. He knew what I wanted, and he offered it to me. Here I am some three and a half decades later, and I can remember and recognize this simple act.

Sometimes I've even risen to the occasion.

A couple of years back I waited on a husband and wife. I chatted with them and found out that he'd recently been diagnosed as celiac. I handed them our gluten-free menu, but I also took the time to talk about modifications of dishes and drinks. They'd already had some problems eating out, so they appreciated the help. It turns out he'd been a real beer nerd. The diagnosis had decimated his favorite hobby. In finding an appropriate drink, I mentioned that many (not all) sakes are gluten-free. Believe it or not, neither of them had heard of sake. I didn't have all the information, but I described the tradition of the drink, and I had him try some. It scratched his itch. At the end of the meal, the wife hugged me, and she wrote a message to the manager. She mentioned how much it meant that they could eat out and that their concerns were both heard and understood.

These are anecdotes. The point is that a good server doesn't make a parent feel any worse about their three foot-asshole of a kid. A good server gives the gluten-free menu to the celiac. It's a great server who is empathetic, and who can assess the situation in real time. A great server tries to understand the causes.

A specific list of things to watch for, and precise ways to respond can't be built in advance (or at least it shouldn't). Being a great server means developing the skills that allow you to be aware and pay attention.

There are many books on service, but the truth is that much of what makes for a great server is learned on the job. The differences between "good" and "great" often result from how specific restaurants function. What's in this book are some guidelines and suggestions, not rules. Rules come from your manager. But take those rules, and these suggestions, and then you have something.

My advice? Be wary of all advice and rules.

The first general manager I ever worked for was shadier than shady, but he taught me a great deal.

I was in college and looking for a new job after a dismal three-week stint at a 24-hour copy shop. Someone in the dorm told me that the restaurant she worked at was, "Hiring anybody!"

That fit me perfectly.

I had a ten-minute interview with this manager. He asked me about my experience, and I was honest. Up until this point I had only ever worked as a magician and a reporter (yes). So I showed him a trick and pleaded for a job. He didn't have room in the restaurant, but my inexperience and enthusiasm appealed to him. He offered me a summer job selling T-shirts.

By the end of the summer, I'd won a few sales contests and maintained my enthusiasm, so he made me a bartender. I had a rocky start. It took me longer than it should have to learn the job. But he told me, "I'd always rather hire someone who doesn't know what they're doing. I want them to do it my way."

Years later, while working as a restaurant manager, I came across a corollary to this theorem. "I can teach anybody anything, except I can't teach anyone to give a fuck." It sounds like something I'd say, but it also sounds like something many others would say. I can't lay claim to this saying, but I wholeheartedly agree with it.

When you go to work in a new restaurant, they always want you to do it their way. They are going to have their set of standards. You have to be willing to adapt to that. Maybe you'll teach them a thing or two, but perhaps you can learn something.

Many of the hard skills are malleable. But a willingness to care about why they do, what they do, the way they do it... that is the unteachable skill. To get to this point, you have to believe that there's value in the work.

This is where I get philosophical. To quote Hippocrates (of "oath" fame), "Let food be thy medicine and medicine be thy food."

Food is important. There are direct links to health, allergies, and sanitation. Food is also a holistic medicine. We use it to soothe all kinds of aches and pains. People "feed a cold," and "drink to forget." It's how people celebrate, mourn, and get to know each other.

There have been only a handful of times where I felt like I improved someone's life by doing what I do. But I get a rush when it happens. From time to time restaurants have improved my life without their knowing it. I hope I've been part of unspoken relief for others.

For such a simple job, it can profoundly affect people.

A few summers ago I worked with Bill, a forty-something force of nature with a "Madonna" tattoo on his forearm. Bill often describes himself as a "career diner waitress." He is excellent at his job.

He often repeats the following (in his thick New York accent) when co-workers stress out: "It's just food and forks!"

He knows more about people than they know about themselves, and he can read anyone like a magazine. Through it all, people love him. He has generations of fans who follow him around from restaurant to restaurant. Bill loves his life, his friends, and he may be the most authentic person I know.

Bill is worth aspiring to. He gives excellent service and just the right amount of fucks.

EXERCISES:

- **Volunteer at a soup kitchen or food bank.** The benefits should be obvious, but the critical takeaway here is empathy. If you can enjoy this kind of work while not making a dime, it's a good sign that this is the job for you. It might even mean that you'd make good money at it.

- **Eat at a terrible restaurant.** I mean it. Go out there, and find the lowest ranked place on Yelp. I don't mean something "overrated." I mean find your local Amy's Baking Company (*Kitchen Nightmares*, Season 6, Episode 16. Best car crash ever.). Concentrate on the feelings that a poor dining experience kick-up. Take the time to understand all the ways that the restaurant fails. Then try to figure out if there were ways they could have recovered and made the experience better.

- **Ask a stupid question.** Empathy trickles down. No matter your level of experience, you need to feel like you can ask questions to your management team. Ask them what you perceive as a "dumb" (within reason) question. See how they handle your stupidity. Did they succeed in not making you feel like a total asshat? Examine how they humored your request. At some point, that will be you fielding a request from a table. If your boss fails, take a closer look at your employment.

- **Learn another language.** Holy shit is this a valuable skill. Estoy tarde a la mesa on this. Now that I've started, I don't think I'll ever stop wanting to learn mas. It opens up your world and forces you to think in new ways. It's empathy on steroids. Plus, it opens up your employment opportunities. There is no downside here.

THE FUCKING BASICS

This is the practical part of waiting tables. This is the "making your bed" chapter. None of it is groundbreaking, but it's all universal.

The job starts with you, your equipment, and your space.

I worked as a bouncer a handful of times in my career, and bouncing demonstrates the necessity of the basics. I didn't much care for the job. Bouncers operate opposite to empathy. Designed to be barriers, they're like a cervical-cap for a bar. They keep out the "spunk."

For starters, I always had to be mentally prepared to turn people away. I always had to be able to say no. Resting bitch face and selective hearing was my bread and butter.

From there, my uniform was built mainly upon the absence of things. No jewelry or long hair. Nothing that dangles and gives assholes something to grab on to. It was recommended that I shave my head and not wear glasses or earrings. Then there's ring avulsion (look it up). Keep extra shit out of your pockets. Phones can break. Keys hurt if you fall on them.

Wear a presentable, but cheap, white, button-down, along with a simple undershirt. A collared shirt gives you the air of authority. But, unlike a polo shirt, a button-down is easier to take off if you're trapped or caught on someone. White is also good because it makes it easier to spot the other bouncers in a dark club or bar. Make sure it's cheap because it may get torn and you'll probably get puked on.

Wear non slip, steel toed, boots. Go for the lightest ones you can find because you might have to run. Know where the ID book, mag lights, keys, and fire extinguishers are. Know all your exits and any extra "entrances."

Preparing for a bouncing shift was like going into a battle. Preparing for the worst made success more accessible. But, that was bouncing.

When it comes to serving, it's better to think about it in terms of tea.

If you want to understand the basics of great serving, look at tea service. It's a simple task that at every restaurant, at every level, is generally considered a pain in the ass.

In the United States, tea is rarely ordered. Then, no matter what's involved in assembling it, it's often just complex enough to mess with a routine. In most restaurants, every other beverage is a one-and-done situation. You stick a cup under a nozzle or place an order with a bartender or barista. Some servers live in espresso machine hell, but that's a whole other book.

Let's examine tea service, and use it to explore a server's basic preparation.

You have the most control of your shift before you hit the floor.

13

Once on the floor, the thing you have the most power over is yourself. So let's start with that and work our way out.

Mindset

What follows involves some heavy stereotyping. Consider the "standard" tea drinker in the United States. It's usually older folks. Often women. Often foreigners. In general, tea is associated with customers labeled as "high-maintenance/low-tip." This means that some have a natural bias against doing more than the minimum for their tea service.

The first step to countering bias is to recognize it. Resist the urge to half-ass your tea service. It's true for tea, and it's true for you too. Acknowledging your biases, opinions, and feelings can be hard. But, when you do, it makes your job easier. In *Setting the Table*, restaurateur Danny Meyer refers to your state of mind as "the weather report." It's all about knowing where your head is at and acting accordingly.

There was a point in my own life when I used my job to avoid other issues. It was an excuse not to think about things. This was unhealthy. It made me moody, irritable, and at the end of one clopen-double[2], I hallucinated. In the middle of my shift, I saw a woman with no eyes. She had two flat flesh panels where her ocular cavities would be. I had to ask someone to check if I had seen what I thought I saw. It was all in my head.

I wasn't checking in with myself, and my brain broke me.

Examine your mental state before going into a shift. Many alcoholics are familiar with the Serenity Prayer. Both the prayer and your shift, are about recognizing what you can change and what you can't. Then you work with what you have left.

If someone orders tea, there's nothing you can do about it. Make it work.

Cleanliness

When it comes to tea, this means checking in on the basics before your first table. Are the teapots clean? Used infrequently, teapots don't always get cleaned properly. Then they get put away dirty. Cleaning in the middle of the shift is such a drain on time. If your restaurant has a tea box or tea basket, is it also clean and presentable? Dusty felt? Splitting wicker? (Two great banjo-band names.) Doing a 10-second check on this stuff before a shift is more convenient than correcting it in service. Strive to make the mid-service process a grab and go situation.

Servers too should be clean enough so that no one has to think about them during service.

I've worked with some people over the years who looked clean but smelled terrible. You weren't thinking about them and then suddenly they were unavoidable. Don't be unavoidable. My cursory research indicates that daily showers do everything from help with depression, to aid in healthy sleep. Showers dry out your skin? Try cocoa butter.

The easy answer seems to be perfume. Don't. The rule is "six inches." Your smell shouldn't extend beyond that range, and within it, you should smell fresh. A guest shouldn't smell you, and a coworker shouldn't care.

Both you and the tea should be ready to make a quick, positive, impression.

Mints

In tea service, this is about knowing your product. I worked at one restaurant where the mint tea was caffeinated, and another where the mint tea was decaf. Most people will assume a mint tea is a pure herbal mix and thus decaffeinated. Caffeine is often a big deal to tea drinkers. Read the packaging and know when to give people the heads up.

When we're talking about servers, let's face it, your mouth is the stink hole from which every part of your job flows. For breath fresheners, I prefer tiny but mighty "tics" and quick dissolve strips. Both discourage tableside chewing.

Be aware of your tea. Be mindful of your breath.

Drink Me, Eat Me

For some people, the process of selecting a tea is akin to choosing a bottle of wine. Even if you don't drink tea, it pays to know a little. Is one of them "sweeter"? Are their strong floral notes? You don't need to be an expert, but being able to confidently offer a recommendation is something worth figuring out. Drink the tea every now and again.

Speaking of having tea before your shift, feeling hungry? Eat something. There are states where breaks are mandated, but it's still not the norm. Can you go without food for eight hours or more?

If you're a fan of intermittent fasting, perfect! But, if you need regular meals - take care of that shit before you start. I find that it helps to think of restaurant work like marathon running. Get in enough nutrition to sustain yourself, but not so much that it weighs you down. There are many quick supplements: Soylent, gu, blocks, beans, and bars. Ramen seasoning packets and a bottle of water were my personal favorite at one point.

Discuss the food policy with management. Be aware of this stuff because it's incredible how much it can/will affect you. I once worked with a spectacular server who would break down in tears if he didn't get his food. Everyone is different, but know what kind of schedule you need, and make arrangements to make it work. Good restaurants will have a food policy in place. Usually, it will include designated snacking areas, etc.

I will say this: beware of nuts. We'll talk about allergies. Enough people have allergies to nuts that your snack shouldn't endanger stranger's lives.

It doesn't matter if you're getting someone tea or a sandwich. The best way to make sure you successfully satisfy others is to be self-satisfied.

That's what he said last night.

The Box / Your Bag

Tea boxes often look like jewelry boxes, hardwood with felt interiors. More often than not they're either too big for the tea selection, or too small to be necessary. Remembering the tea selection might be easier than fetching the box and waiting for Edna to flip through it.

That said, this is an opportunity to diversify your options. Give yourself the ability for alternate approaches. For some people, bringing over the box will produce an "Oooh." It's a bit of theater that enhances the experience. Sometimes you don't have time for that nonsense. If you can guide your tea aficionado verbally, that's another arrow in your quiver. If you cleaned and prepped the box before the shift, maybe you can leave the box at the table, which gives you the chance to walk away.

Figure out the best ways to use the box while not relying on it. Consider your options and have a backup plan in place that will allow you to switch up your game in the moment.

When it comes to the server, this is about the bag you take to work. It's often an afterthought, but it's also your backup. Depending on the uniform, I almost always like to have a full spare in there. I also try to keep an extra deodorant stick, a power bar, mints, some spare cash, and backup pens too.

I used to work at the Cheesecake Factory back when the uniforms were all white. One time I had an entire container of balsamic vinaigrette spill down my front. With no backup, I had to go home. Not having a uniform backup cost me money. Another time, while riding to work on the bus, I sat in poop. Luckily my significant other brought me extra pants. This "shitcident," convinced me to keep an entire spare outfit with me. A spare uniform makes it easier to deal with unexpected doubles or last-minute shift pickups.

Whether it's tea or your basic equipment — give yourself options.

Multitasking

The key "problem" with tea service is that it takes time. Being aware that this will take extra time is part of the deal. Accept it.

Once the tea is selected, ask them how they take it (lemon, milk, sugar, etc.), and then, start the process.

Charge the mug (heat it using hot water). I'm surprised at how often this impresses hardcore tea drinkers. It obviously doesn't happen often.

If it's loose tea, know the appropriate amount of tea. Know appropriate steeping time. Even if you're serving Lipton, make an effort to give them the best cup of Lipton possible.

When you drop off the tea, do you provide a spoon, saucer, ramekin, monkey dish, or some other form of tea bag receptacle? Let them know how much longer it has to go. Some people like strong tea. Some people like weak tea.

If you drop off honey, how is the honey getting out of its container? Did they ask for lemon? Milk? Both?

This can feel like a lot of extra tasks, but it's a matter of anticipating needs. A good server brings everything to the table with the tea (milk and lemon and honey and sugar). But the great server finds a way to have the conversation in advance and only brings out what's necessary.

But there's even more to it.

Early in my serving career, I had a young American fellow order both milk and lemon with his tea. He poured in the milk and squirted it with lemon. It instantly curdled. He called me over saying, "Your milk is bad. This never happens at home."

I went through the process again with a brand new container of milk. It happened again. Now he was frustrated. I had also wasted my time. And, by his estimation, the restaurant didn't look so hot either. The third round was honey and lemon only.

If I had considered the process in advance, the whole thing could have been avoided.

At the time I didn't understand the basics of tea. *The Kitchn* editor and fermentation expert Emma Christensen (@ChristensenEmma) explains the science:

> *"Normally, little groupings of casein float around in the milk without bonding to anything. These groupings (technically called micelles) have a negative charge, which makes them repel other groupings of casein and keeps the casein evenly dispersed in the milk. When milk becomes too acidic, like when we add lemon juice or when it goes sour, the negative charge on the casein groupings becomes neutralized. Now instead of pushing each other apart, the casein starts to clump together. Eventually, large enough clumps are formed that we can actually see the separation, and then we have curdled milk."*

It turns out if the milk is hot, the curling happens even faster. On the other hand, heavy cream or half-and-half, "can handle the addition of [an acid] without so much as a casein clump."

In other words, I could have avoided the hassle. With more knowledge, I could have discussed his options in advance. I could have offered him half-and-half, which was what he was probably using at home.

What does that have to do with "Multitasking" (the title of this section)?

Every restaurant job post lists multitasking as a top requirement of the job. The problem? Science says multitasking doesn't exist.

In 2008 NPR reported, "Don't believe the multitasking hype, scientists say... we [actually] switch our attention from task to task extremely quickly." After that, many articles cited a 2015 University of London study. This study says that multitasking has effects similar to smoking marijuana. It drops one's IQ by 15 points and reduces adults to the cognitive abilities of an 8-year-old.

Then, in 2017, *Entrepreneur* magazine put out an article: "Why Smart People Don't Multitask." They add in a study from the University of Sussex, "They found that high multitaskers had less brain density in the anterior cingulate cortex, a region responsible for empathy as well as cognitive and emotional control."

That sucks because empathy and emotional control are two essential parts of this job. The Essex study goes on to say that some of the damage seems to be permanent.

Well shit. Is there an alternative to multitasking?

One significant alternative to multitasking is anticipating needs. Understanding the natural flow of events, and managing them in short order looks a lot like "multitasking."

There are other multitasking alternatives too.

"Be selective of what you agree to do." is a frequent multi-tasking alternative geared towards office types. But any server should also know their limits. Saying "No" is something that you have to be able to do. You also need to be able to say it before getting so overwhelmed that your "no," becomes an act of violence. This means knowing when to ask for help.

Another piece of advice for multitaskers? "Minimize interruptions." This is hard in a restaurant. Instead, be able to prioritize who you listen to, and gauge how serious to take a request.

Oh, and don't bring your phone on the floor. It's not worth it.

Another curious "multitasking" alternative I came across? "Have brief and focused meetings." It's important to know how to have brief conversations with people. Get to the point. No equivocation. Sometimes it means forgoing niceties. With co-workers, be direct with a smile. Try with all your might to use the magic words, and (in turn) don't take abrupt requests personally.

Something that kept my sanity over the years was being able to have conversations with coworkers that spanned the duration of the shift. Each part of the discussion might only be a sentence, and there'd be long gaps between each thought. One interesting talk like this involved Gun's and Roses "Sweet November Rain." My co-worker claimed it was the greatest song of its generation. My position was, "hell, no."

Using a series of two-second sentences, back and forth, over the course of a shift, we decided that I was correct.

Lastly, there's "focus on one task at a time." This is the hardest, but it's also the most important. In a 2011 article in *The Atlantic* writer Derek Thompson suggests that multitasking exists, but that it's not about rapid-fire concentration. Instead, he posits, it's actually about finding the value in following distractions.

I think he's correct in a way. It's about following the right distractions. In that case, the skill we're talking about isn't multitasking; it's prioritizing.

Getting someone the perfect cup of tea involves anticipating what they'll need. Then it's about knowing what they want even if they are unsure (by having the right conversation). Then it's about knowing exactly how to deliver on it.

With that, you have multitasked your way to a perfect cuppa. Me? I drink black coffee.

Let's drop the tea, and get to some other nuts and bolts.

Wear a decent uniform. Pants, shirts, ties, vests - all of this is restaurant dependant. Most long-term staffers swap and trade tips on how to maintain the look. Team Febreeze or Team Downey? Scotchgard.

What about shoes?

The Shoes

Comfortable is king, but nonslip is non-negotiable. I also prefer a smooth "leather" exterior that's easy to clean. The worst shoes I had to deal with were the white-nightmare of The Cheesecake Factory. The floors there were slippery and hard enough that they could kill you as fast as the food. At the time the only white, nonslip, shoes I could find were sneakers. This meant cleaning them with a toothbrush and shellacking them with shoe whitener every night. They built up crusty layers of "paint," and at some point even when they were clean they looked dirty.

The Apron

I both love and loathe aprons. They are crazy useful, but they inherently look like a fanny pack without a zipper. I have at least two for any job. Something to consider is that they last longer if you spot clean them as opposed to tossing them blindly in the wash.

The Book

Some people have lovely books they get in a stationary store. Durable and effective. Others cobble together things like old check presenters, cardboard, and scrap paper. I'm in the second camp. Are you working in a nice restaurant? Keep up the illusion with a book that looks nice, at least on the outside.

Books often get lost, fall into toilets, etc. I try not to keep anything of value in them while working. Instead, keep a labeled cup (or a second book) with credit slips and cash at a service station. I remember the summer I worked in a restaurant built on a boat dock. A coworker lost a customer's black AMEX through the cracks of the dock.

Let that guy be your cautionary tale.

A NOTE ON NOTES: I always recommend writing down orders — paper trail. But how you write that order is personal. Everyone writes them differently. That said, there's a benefit to writing legibly. It means that in an emergency, you can pass off the order to a third party to input for the kitchen. This is handy if you're bogged down in a tea service...

Pens

Leakproof black or leakproof blue. Did I mention leakproof? I also recommend having a sharpie. Everyone in the kitchen has one, why not you? They also help in dating open wine bottles, milk jugs, etc.

Remember: Lending out a writing implement out is equivalent to throwing it in the trash.

Wine Opener

Have a good wine opener. That is a subjective description because my perfect wine opener was a pain for most folks to use. I never had a problem, but to everyone else, it was clunky and awkward. Coworkers refused to borrow it. Rude perhaps, but I was never without a wine opener.

Other servers befriend wine distributors and accumulate many decent, branded, double-hinged corkscrews. Regardless of my preferences, I'll always recommend a covetable, double hinge, opener. Quick and smooth wine service is worth striving for.

Utility Knife / Leatherman / Churchkey

I used to keep a swiss army card on me that had on it a ruler, a toothpick, and scissors. Having this, or a Leatherman or even an old-fashioned churchkey means you can pop open a bottle at a moment's notice. This is a great ability even if you're not a bartender. Screwdrivers help with espresso machines, cleaning french presses, and fixing wobbly furniture. Big, chunky, classic churchkeys are great for breaking down boxes and eye gouging.

Table Numbers

Earlier I mentioned that learning a language helps cultivate empathy. That idea comes from a TED talk by cognitive scientist Lera Boroditsky. In "How language shapes the way we think," she references the Kuuk Thaayorre, an indigenous Australian tribe. Their native language is based on cardinal directions (North, South, East, West). For them, every interaction starts with labeling direction. Everything they do is described in that context.

Table numbers are the foundation for restaurants. In a room of 200 assorted people, a table number ensures a person gets what they ordered. Table numbers direct the bulk of servers' actions.

In an odd quirk, you may also find that specific tables seem to direct customers' behavior.

At one restaurant, table-44 was known as the "make-out table." It happened there almost every night. Of course, the table's location plays a part in that behavior. In this case, it was a two-top wedged into a dark corner. Since this was a busy restaurant, it was sat at least once in the first round of dinner service due to convenience. Because of that timing, it was also usually sat at the start of the prime dinner hour.

These facts combined to make table-44 a semi-secluded two top available during the date-night-dinner-hour. Hence, smoo-chie-bootchies.

Now you quickly understand a few things about the table without even seeing it. It's a two-top. It's a semi-awkward table to get to, and as such, there's a good chance a busser has not visited them. They might need water or need dishes cleared. I know that if I'm delivering one dish to the table, there's a good chance it's being shared.

A lot of this isn't conscious thinking. You'll quickly identify that certain tables are "undesirable." As such, anyone stuck sitting there might be on the surly side of things. Table numbers will start to dictate how you prepare to approach people.

But, there's a much simpler reason to lean those digits.

The second-worst restaurant I ever worked at came at a time in my life when I was having a hard time checking my troubles at the door. The place also had a nightmare chef. Then, one night I forgot my table numbers, and I ran food to the wrong table. All hell broke loose. No one died, but I wished I had. It was the worst that I've ever felt in a restaurant.

Know your table numbers cold. Know them so well that you couldn't forget them if you tried.

Seat Numbers

Knowing a table number is like knowing you're going to Texas. A seat number is the difference between winding up in Austin or Lubbock.

One way to make people feel special and unique is to reduce them to a number. Something that often irritates people is when a server asks, "Who gets this item?" People want to believe that they are memorable and unique, even when they aren't. Seat numbers may be the most practical way to reassure guests that you know what's going on, even if you don't.

The rule I'm familiar with is that "seat one" is closest to the kitchen. Then the numbers continue around the table clockwise. Restaurants sometimes have variations on this rule for unusually shaped dining rooms. If your restaurant has a system, take the time to learn it.

Even if you're the only one using these numbers, being able to recall which seat ordered what can help you, it means *you* always know who got which burger toppings -- even when they forget.

Sightlines / Acoustics

Much like gender, large parts of restaurants are performative. As such, restaurants have parts that are "onstage" and parts that are "offstage." Know the appropriate place to talk about your jock-itch. In doubt? Hush. Hush. Keep it down now. Voices carry.

Know Your Brand

Knowing what image the bosses want to present "onstage" is essential. A lot of smaller, higher-end restaurants build a following based on a particular image. Sometimes they want the server to have a casual customer relationship. Sometimes they don't. I once worked in a restaurant that was pretty casual, but listed the following rules:

- No crouching at the table
- No leaning
- No using introducing yourself at the table.

Years ago I was told that the first two help increase tips. In chain restaurants, I was often expected to introduce myself by name. I did all three without thinking. It took an effort to make these new rules a part of my new "natural approach."

Ultimately people choose the restaurant, not the server. Be the best server for the restaurant you work in.

Detailing

When I started in restaurants, I was taught to look at my tables as real estate. I was then allowed to make money off of that "space" during business hours. At this point, the entirety of my income came through my tips (no pooling, no paycheck). Every dollar I made was due to how well I maintained my real estate. I look back at this view as rather cut-throat. It implied no loyalty to my fellow servers and little loyalty to the restaurant itself.

But it drilled in certain realities.

It meant managing and detailing my section was up to me. No wobbly tables (yes to "wobble wedges" - no to "napkin wads"). It meant playing an active role in setting up large party tables. I learned that alcohol removes water spots. Vinegar is smelly but makes things less sticky and baking soda helps with stains. I learned that when wearing shorts, crumbs on a vinyl banquet feels like sitting on a wet toilet seat. Pens and markers can help "repair" scratched wooden tables and damaged vinyl seats.

I also suggest sitting in the seats occasionally. Sometimes it reveals unknown sight-lines, sticky tables, or other quirks you hadn't noticed. It also teaches you how irritating the wobbly table is.

Think of sitting at the table as someone walking into your house for the first time. Even before you show up to welcome them, they're judging you by the state of your tables. Fix the nonsense.

Backups

Know where all your backup supplies are. Check in on levels before a shift (even if it's not your job). For example, has the tea been stocked? If you're feeling ambitious, find out where your serviceware comes from. More than a few times people have asked me where they can buy something like the dishes, plates, or where we get our tea. If you already know the answers, it prevents you from having to run around for that info at the worst possible time. Plus it makes you look like an expert, and gives you authority.

Also, write down when things get low and tell a manager, even if it's not part of your side work. It may seem like a hassle, and the manager may also act like it is, but you know that feeling when you run out of toilet paper? That's the kind of frustration you'll feel at 9 PM on a Saturday when you suddenly have no chamomile tea.

Server Stations

Keeping server stations clean and organized is vital. They are communal spaces, and the more organized they are, the quicker they are to navigate. Also, they're usually more "onstage" than servers realize.

The Floor Map

Look at the service map, and gage who is working in the sections around you. It won't take long for you to discover which servers are helpful and which ones lose their shit. Sometimes your "weather report" will dictate that working next to Tori will hinder you. In that case, it might be worth finagling a section-switch for everyone's sanity.

It also means that if a random table flags you down you already know that it's in Tori's section. That way you can quickly put the order in for her. For those interested, I have changed the name of every former coworker in this book except for Tori.

Tori knows why.

See the Whole Room

Once you understand yourself, your equipment, and the layout, you'll be able to, "see the whole room."

Part of this involves using your peripheral vision. It means being aware of everything that's happening even if you're not engaged in it. A big part of this is about being self-aware. That's a lot easier if all the little things are taken care of, and you don't overwhelm your focus. But, it also means putting yourself in a position where you see as much of what is going on as you can.

I have a kind of "peripheral vision system." It's a series of default tasks dictated by where I am in the restaurant. Each task then leads me to the next task and so on. These spots vary from restaurant to restaurant but they usually revolve around this cycle.

KITCHEN: This is my first fall-back position. Running food is always a top priority. I've never worked for a chef that wasn't keeping a mental score of who came to the pass. They are a.) keeping track of who is running food and b.) plotting the death of those who fly by looking for their own food but who never run other food in the window.

DISH: If I'm near the kitchen, I'm usually also near the dish room. If there's no food to run, I look for serviceware that needs to go back into circulation. There's usually something that can go back out on the floor. Taking the clean stuff out keeps everyone prepared. It also gives you an excuse to walk past your section and the...

SERVER STATION: Is it clean? Pens? Check presenters? Stocked? Extra menus? I usually also do a pat down of myself at this point. Have I collected pens that would better serve the world here? Typically, server stations are in central locations, at least one of which is in view of...

SERVICE BAR: Drinks to run? Is the barback swamped? Do bottles need to be pulled from the wine room? Do they need ice? Check in and say hi. Then grab those extra menus tucked behind the bar server station, and bring them to...

HOST: Help them out with menus and seating where you can. Often hosts are the last to get assistance, so be their knight in shining armor.

BATHROOMS: This is often a "host job." But, maybe the host is tired of checking in on the drunk bachelor/bachelorette. Perhaps you need to pee? While you're in there, how's it looking? New graffiti? No TP? Take an inventory, because everyone there to eat dinner will. Then wash your hands...

Rinse. Repeat. As I make these rounds, I'm walking through my section, and gauging table's progress.

Want to make this whole process easy to remember? Just remember the phrase, "Full hands in. Full hands out." In other words, never go somewhere empty handed and keep your eyes open as you do it.

EXERCISES:

- **Read.** Much has been written about the intricacies of working in a restaurant. A great deal of it is anecdotal and includes titles like *Waiter Rant* by Steve Dublanica. Then there's *Waiting: The True Confessions of a Waitress* by Debra Ginsberg. For tips on hospitality, read *Setting the Table* By Danny Meyer. It may be the closest thing this industry has to a New Testament. *Clam Chowder: The Server's Field Manual* is a short guide I read years ago by a man named Matt Lehman. It has lots of stories, and from what I remember some good practical tips. One book I've not read, but that comes recommended is *Front of the House: Restaurant Manners, Misbehaviors & Secrets* by Jeff Benjamin.

- **Watch YouTube.** There's some crap on there, but there's also some good advice mixed in. I wouldn't spend hours doing this, but search "how to wait tables." You'll find people from all over giving a wide variety of tips and tricks. I spent hours watching videos. For simple, quick, and useful, my favorite was, "5 Tips To Be A Better Server, Increase Your Tips & Make More Money Now!" by Emily Anderson. I recommend YouTube because it's a constant stream of so many voices that it stays more up to date than any book. This has its drawbacks of course. Part of being a great server is learning how to filter good information from the bad stuff. YouTube is nothing if not a massive pile of... stuff.

- **Read the training manual.** Not every restaurant has one, but if they do, read it. A lot of this kind of information came to me through the standard training materials. I wouldn't say that they are all invaluable, but they help you understand the image the restaurant is trying to project.

- **Eat in your restaurant.** Honestly, not everyone can swing this, but if you can afford a bite in your place of employment, go in and eat. If it's the kind of place where you have to make a reservation, don't do it under your name. If you're given the option, sit in the section of a more "seasoned" server. Take in the atmosphere from that point of view. Watch how people move on the floor. Listen carefully to how your server uses language and presentation. Order a tea. Don't forget that you will need to leave a good tip.

- **Make a list of 50 tasks.** This might be a better task for two or more people, but assemble a list of 50 potential tasks in the restaurant. This can range from the pedantic ("greet table 25") to the rare ("cut off a drunk at the bar"). Put in everything from, make tea, to restock napkins, clean table 120, to seat a party of four. The idea is to make a list of 50 random tasks that you might possibly have to handle. Then prioritize that list from 1 through 50. You will probably never have to make a list like this in your serving career, but think about how you prioritize and why you prioritize it the way that you do.

THE FUCKING RESTAURANT

"If you know the enemy and know yourself, you need not fear the result of a hundred battles."

- SUN TZU, THE ART OF WAR

It's helpful to know what you're doing.

Some people know little about food and beverage but wait tables and do it well. Everyone eats and drinks. Everyone has a bare minimum of relevant experience. This is one of those times when even amateurs are experts (to an extent).

Once upon a time, I had a discussion with my general manager about a customer's dairy allergy. He told me they couldn't make them a certain dish because the sauce had mayonnaise in it. He clarified that there were eggs in the mayonnaise.

I stopped, confused, and said that eggs weren't dairy. He assured me that they were.

I was about to point out that dairy came from mammals and almost said something like, "I could milk a goddamn whale before you could milk a fucking chicken."

But, as I opened my mouth, he cut me off with, "Mayonnaise is 'creamy,' and you buy eggs in the dairy aisle, no?"

I shut it. This man ran a successful restaurant. He made six fig-ures. There was nothing I could say in that moment that was going to change his mind.

It's good if you can do it, but this job isn't about identifying genuine wagyu, or knowing what makes authentic paella. It's about recognizing that a server is a piece in a machine. Excelling at your job is about determining how best to make tab "a" fit into slot "b."

Transferring to another metaphor, waiting tables is the tip of an enormous iceberg. Let's break down the restaurant and get a better idea of what's under the surface.

Let us milk a whale together.

The Kitchen

There was a point where I didn't know understand restaurants at all. I remember once going to a bar and asking the bartender, "What's your cheapest beer?"

I remember him rolling his eyes. Hard.

For a long time, the biggest mystery for me was the kitchen. I knew some basics, but I didn't understand how restaurant cook-ing worked. I didn't understand the life cycle of food. I didn't ap-preciate what things cost in terms of time or money, and I didn't appreciate how things got processed. I put in an order and out came food. I knew specific orders upset the kitchen, but I didn't understand why.

Over time I got to know the cooks. We smoked weed together in the freight elevator. I had drinks with them after work. I lived with them. I found out that I loved kitchen people as much, if not more than the front of house folks. Eventually, I even tran-sitioned from the front of the house to the back of the house. It was an eye-opening experience.

Even though I wound up back in the front of the house, working in the kitchen is what made me a capable server.

There is a difference in the skills necessary for success in the kitchen versus the floor. But, if the two groups don't understand what the others are doing, it's hard to move the restaurant forward.

The most significant difference between the server and the cook is the direction of osmosis.

Servers are hired because the restaurant wants to absorb their warmth and personality. Server's have to, "be the best version of themselves."

Cooks have to, "be the best version of the Chef." The whole idea is that cooks do their jobs as much like her as possible. The Chef needs each cook to absorb her skills and standards for a specific task.

The cook is about making the restaurant look good. The server is about making the guest feel good. A server needs to be able to explain to a customer that the bacon mayo is not vegetarian and do it with a smile. The cook can laugh at the server for asking the same question. Servers focus on emotional labor and cooks focus on physical labor. The server is ego to the cook's id.

The back of the house is concrete and results-oriented. Everything has to get done in a specific way by a particular time. Servers deal with deadlines too, but not in the same way. A cook's job is to meet deadlines. A server's job is to manage them.

One big challenge is that most servers make more than most cooks while working fewer hours. For me, there was a point where I couldn't keep working in kitchens because I couldn't financially sustain it. This is a big problem. It has been known to drive a wedge between these two groups of people who need to be able to work together.

As long as this disparity exists, as a server, your job is to counter that friction. Make an honest effort to understand what it is that they do, and how they do it. Make their jobs as easy as you can.

Where do you start?

Read your menu and know it cold. Make flashcards. If you can, order off the menu as much as possible, and look at the ingredients. Make a game out of it, and try to write down every element in a dish, even if it's a cheeseburger. This might seem difficult if you don't cook, but knowing that the bun is toasted, or that it comes with mayo, is a start.

Google, "mayonnaise recipe." Then Google, "are eggs dairy?"

We live in a world where if you have a phone, you can watch someone make mayonnaise anywhere at any time. If you're serving the food, take the time to watch someone make it. You don't have to be able to make it; you only need to have an idea of what you're serving. A cook laughs at a server when they ask something that seems obvious to them because it's their entire world.

You need to appreciate that cooks have stress dreams about making mayo.

It's also frustrating when you work with someone who profits off your work but doesn't understand what you do.

I suppose; next, you could read *Blood, Bones & Butter* or *Prune* by Gabrielle Hamilton. Or Bourdain's *Kitchen Confidential*, *Medium Raw* and *The Nasty Bits*. Or even *The Making of a Chef* and *Soul of a Chef* by Michael Ruhlman.

But frankly, the reading is less critical. Do something.

Learn the kitchen brigade system and try to understand how your kitchen compares. Not every restaurant is laid out the same. What one restaurant calls "Garde Manger" is "The Salad

Station" somewhere else.

Once you have an idea of the positions, watch your kitchen work. If your restaurant offers food runner shifts, pick one up. Watch the food expeditor call out orders, and try to follow the process a dish goes through to get to the window. Watch how a ticket comes to completion.

While you're running, watch the cooks. They are looking at a rail of tickets all while trying to hold a combination of augmentations in their head. They are tracking cooking times, resource levels, special requests, and trying not to kill people with food allergies. The job is like juggling while bicycling. It's expected without question that they get from point a to point b without dropping any balls or crashing.

A clown gets a round of applause for doing that.

Ask the chef if you can "Stage" or "Trail." They'll most likely put you with a prep cook. There you'll do something annoying, repetitive, and possibly inconsequential. They want to mitigate the damage you can do. Once I worked with a server who staged and mangled a service's worth of imported white asparagus. The lesson here? Pay attention.

Clean, green beans for 30 minutes, and you'll start thinking about every order of green beans that goes out.

Do you know what all this is? Kitchen empathy.

I worked as a baker and pastry assistant for a small, high-end restaurant. I got to work each day between 4 AM and 5 AM, and depending on the day I worked until about 1 PM or 2 PM. My most favorite people in the world were the servers who came in just as I was wrapping up and offered to get me a coffee. Be that server. See one of the cooks out at the bar after work? Buy them a beer. You can afford it. Talk to them, and ask them questions. Get to know them, thank them for everything they do for you, and let them know if people complimented the food.

You'll learn a lot as you work, but achieving a high level of knowledge and expertise isn't a requirement. I've watched Bobby Flay repeatedly say that you sear meat to, "seal in the juices." Flay is definitely an expert. At the same time, I have read Harold McGee, and I know that "sealing in the juices" is not a real thing. You don't have to be infallible to be good at the job, and you're not Bobby Flay.

The important thing is to ask questions. Once you take the time to get to know the cooks in your kitchen, it's a lot easier to ask them questions.

But no. Eggs are not fucking dairy.

EXERCISES:

- **Read, memorize, and understand your menu.** The first two parts of that are self-explanatory. That last part is what ups your game. Try to understand the food that's being served. How would you describe a dish to someone with no point of reference? If someone asks you for a dish that's, "like a hamburger" what would you recommend? Figure out how to describe more complicated dishes or techniques in simpler terms, i.e., (Aioli - "It's like a lighter, smoother mayonnaise with garlic.")

- **Make cookies.** Making cookies for the kitchen is a simple way to say thank you. If you are a terrible baker, even bringing them in something you buy is a lovely "thank you." They do get tired of eating the food that they make. Plus, offering them snacks, also gives you an opportunity to learn and memorize their favorite coffee/tea/drink orders.

- **"Song Exploder" a dish.** In the killer podcast, *Song Exploder* host Hrishikesh Hirway takes apart a song with the writer and examines all its elements. Pull apart a dish in the same way. Learn its history. Who created it? Where did the spice blend it uses come from? Even if you work at a Friday's, there is a story behind everything. Just look up the history of the potato skin (*Eater* did a great breakdown). If you work in a joint with a "Chef," talk to them about their dish. Some customers will want to engage on that level.

- **Kitchen stage.** Not every restaurant will want you back there, but it's so worth it. You get to know the kitchen, you learn how things get made, and maybe they'll make you a snack (it's worth it for the snacks).

The Bar

According to Tinder, "Bartender" is one of the best professions to have listed on your profile. Let's face it; it's much sexier to say that you're a bartender than it is to say you're a waiter. But being a bartender isn't necessarily glamorous.

In many restaurants, a bartender is the first front of the house staff member to get there in the morning. They might also be the last of the staff to leave at night. Through it all, bartenders are responsible for lots of extra work that servers enjoy.

On top of it all, frequently the job involves being on high alert.

People are always trying to break the law at the bartender's expense. I know bartenders whose lives were ruined by serving someone without proper ID. It sucks when you're responsible for other people's poor choices. As such, the bartender's job is vital for any server to understand.

In the morning the bar stocks ice and sets up equipment. They also often squeeze juices, make mixes and syrups, and prepare garnishes. They stock and restock throughout the day — all while waiting on customers. Then at night, they have to wait for the drunks to leave. They do this as they break down, clean, and manage the restaurant's cash.

Bartending is a job that's part back of the house and part front of the house. It requires taking orders and entertaining customers. It also means making drinks for servers who often appear ungrateful or unaware. I've been fortunate to work with a wide variety of great bartenders. They all had different strengths. Neither cooks nor bartenders are monolithic in their skill sets. But, with bartenders, the differences can be dramatic.

There are bartenders whose strength lies in charming customers. I worked with one guy whose nickname was "Nine-Eleven" because he was, "a disaster from New York." He didn't know any drink recipes. He hated servers. He was also slow, and if he worked a day shift, the evening bartenders had to come in early to do extra work to make it through the night.

But, bar customers loved him. He had a thick accent, and he told the funniest stories. If people ordered something complicated, he would say, "What?! No one's drinking mojitos! What you want is a Jack and Coke!"

We sold out of Jack Daniels all the time.

Then some bartenders understand what makes a great cocktail. I've worked with a few in the States who didn't even speak English well. They may only work the service bar, and they often hate dealing with customers. That was Diego. Diego saved his bartending money, eventually bought a big rig and became a long haul trucker.

Then there was Dave. Other bartenders hated working with Dave, and Dave hated working with them. Again, he was decent with customers, but his particular skill set involved prep. He loved cutting fruit and making mixes. He also operated as a management surrogate. He knew every rule and requirement of the corporate offices. His value was in keeping costs low, and stuff prepped.

There's room for all of this, but great bartenders balance all these different skills.

Often bartenders come across as surly or intimidating to servers, and there's a good reason for this. Like the kitchen, servers make money off of the bartender's work. Unlike the kitchen, bartenders often have a better idea of how much their work is worth. Servers work shorter hours, do less physical labor, and yet they often make more than the bartenders.

That last part isn't hard and fast. There are restaurants where the bartenders make considerable cash. There are also bars where they use barbacks who do a lot of the prep work, stocking, and more. More than once I've worked at bars where the barbacks had the hardest jobs. Almost universally those barbacks made less than the servers.

This part of the book is dedicated to a barback I worked with in LA, Juan. I have never depended on another human in a work environment as much as I depended on Juan. If enough people buy this book, I will happily buy Juan his own restaurant.

So, how does one achieve "bar empathy?"

It's the same as with the kitchen. Learn the drink menu. Run drinks. Do some research. Ask questions. Get to know your bartenders. Bring them coffee and cookies. Find out what can help them in the middle of the shift.

When I got my first bartending job, I wasn't a drinker, and I knew almost nothing about alcohol. I had friends who worked at the Friday's down the street so I would take my Mr. Boston guide there and flip to random pages. They had me try drink, after drink, after drink...

One night I started drinking at five and was falling off my stool by eight. At that point, I excused myself, went home, and took a shower.

My girlfriend found me, passed out in a still running, ice cold, shower when she got home... past midnight.

Don't learn the bar that way.

EXERCISES:

- **Stage.** This can be touchy because with the bar you're dealing with a combination of cash registers and alcohol. This can make both bartenders and management touchy. But if you're willing to come in early and help a bartender set up, you'll learn a buttload and make a friend for life. A friend who also happens to know 101 hangover cures.

- **Drink at five bars and get the same drink five times.** Maybe you can crawl this out in a night, but it might make more sense to keep tasting notes and compare it over time. I'd suggest trying this with a cocktail frequently ordered at your place of business. Or, pick a standard classic like a Margarita, Old Fashioned, Sazerac or Negroni.

- **Ask a bartender to recommend a cocktail.** Do this while your out, as a follow up to the five-time beverage. Or ask the bartenders you work with what cocktails they love to make and/or order themselves.

- **Buy a liquor on sale and experiment.** There's a lot of bad liquors, and they don't always sell. When that happens, they often get put on sale. That's your opportunity to experiment. Take that shit home, and see if you can't find a recipe online that utilizes it. Try that recipe, try to understand why it works, or doesn't work. Then, experiment. Recognize that you might be too drunk to judge how good your drinks are.

- **Read a recipe book or *Liquor.com*.** You could pour through a copy of Mr. Boston, but there are better ways to gain insight without falling off a stool or winding up in a four-hour-shower. Liquor.com will keep you up to date with trends, and give you some of the cocktail and liquor history.

- **WINE! BEER!** If you work in a restaurant with a sommelier or cicerone, take advantage of their expertise. Steward a bottle of wine or beer, and learn how to describe it. There are many books and websites devoted to doing this. Take the time to learn.

Dishwashing

At some point in the history of restaurants, you could pay for a meal by washing dishes. After a while, it became a kind of cliché, and you'd see it on TV shows or in cartoons. I don't know when that happened, but that was a very different time.

If you have spent any time in a restaurant, you know that this is bullshit bonkers. The idea that a restaurant would put a civilian in the dish pit is insane. This is an area that has the potential to be the busiest and the most dangerous part of the restaurant. There are broken glasses, hot things, and other hazardous and pointy aspects to this job.

I still have burn scars on my hands from when I started in the kitchen as a dishwasher.

Taking care of a dishwasher is good for you, and it's good for your soul. Get them drinks (water, soda) and make sure that they are well hydrated. When you swing through with full arms or a bus tub, clean off your plates, and treat these people with respect.

Understand that what they do is important. A restaurant cannot operate without a dishwasher. I'd say stage with the dishwasher, but you would very likely get in their way.

EXERCISES:

- **Take a ServSafe course.** If you work with food or sanitation, you should take this course. In some instances, it will help a restaurant's insurance rates. It will also make you more aware of the simple dangers that dishwashers and kitchen people have to be mindful of.

- **Watch a video on dishwasher repair.** Go to the dish room, and see if you can find the brand name and model number of your dishwasher. Write it down, or take a picture with your phone. Then grab a glass of wine. Curl up on the couch, and settle in with YouTube. Google the name and model number. Learn about how to help work/clean/maintain that machine. Maybe it will send you to sleep, or perhaps it'll make you one of the most valuable employees in the restaurant.

- **Read "The Cook's Companions."** It feels unnecessary to mention the work of Anthony Bourdain repeatedly, but this is a story from his collection *The Nasty Bits*, and it is particularly relevant. It also references the George Orwell book, *Down and Out in Paris and London*, which is the next thing you should read.

- **Bake some cookies.** Not only will all these cookies bring you closer to understanding your kitchen team, but it'll also bring you closer to the dishwasher. You might be surprised at how often the dishwasher makes the best food in the restaurant. As a cook, I used to buy all sorts of snacks off the dishwasher. Be on their good side.

Busser/Backwaiter

I want to dedicate this part to Rogie. Rogie was from Brazil. There he was a dental parts supplier. In the States, he worked construction and bussed tables. When I worked with him, he was in his 60s, and that was 20 years ago. I have no idea if he is still alive, but he was the greatest busser I have ever known. Every night that he worked, my job was easier, and because of that, I made more money.

Bussing is a task that is important but gets put off like, "anyone can do it." I can assure you that this is not the case. The reality is that you should be able to do their job better than them, and if you can't, you still have a lot to learn as a server.

If you can't guess, one of my biggest peeves on the floor is when servers treat back waiters like servants. These people don't work for servers. These people work with servers.

An important skill to work on with your bussers or backwaiters is to learn how to communicate with them. I mean this both as a coworker and as a friend. You are two sides to a coin. The standard obstacles are usually two-fold: language and experience.

If it's a language barrier, make an effort to learn the basics. Yes, there's "spoon," "fork," and "knife," but start with "Please," "Thank You," "Pardon me," and "Sorry." Use these words sincerely and please don't be a ding-dong.

A lot of back waiters and bussers are younger folks who don't understand why they are doing what they are doing. They don't know that some people tip based on whether their water glasses remain full. They are thrown by the fact that many gabachos grab their arm and think everyone speaks English.

In some ways, it's your job to teach them how to do your job. You should make it part of your job to communicate what you need and why you need it. If you have an interest in moving up in a restaurant, inspire a bored backwaiter to care about what they're doing.

EXERCISES:

- **Work a Busser Shift.** If you can work a busser shift, and you're the best busser on the floor, then maybe you are ready to wait tables. Don't just steamroll the other bussers either. These are your coworkers. Respect their workspace. Also, ask them for tips on how you can improve, and don't be indignant when they answer.

- **Cocktails and snacks.** Invite them out for a beer — unless they are underage. In that case, get them snacks. Cookies? Find out more about them. Take the time to get to know the people you work closest to on the floor.

- **Ask them if they want to be a waiter.** When thinking about your development and advancement, consider theirs. Out of all the people in the restaurant, these are the people you might be able to help advance. Learn how to advocate for these people and if they are interested, encourage them to move up. They will do a better job if you give them a reason to, "give a fuck."

Host

In thinking of ways to better understand this skill set, my first thought was to suggest putting together a puzzle while someone's yelling at you. I don't think this is a good way to learn anything useful, but I do think that it kind of sums up the host's job.

The host is the restaurant's conductor. They dictate the pace at which people sit down, so they affect the servers, and, in turn, the kitchen. They are also the first person customers interact with. This means they are the ones who have to make someone feel okay about waiting an hour for a table.

Being put in this position means that often hosts feel like everyone is out to get them.

The guests get pissed at hosts because they have to wait for tables. Then the servers chew out the hosts for triple seating them. This then backs-up the kitchen, so the kitchen gets grumpy at the managers. Then the cycle repeats.

Hosts are often the people in the restaurant with the least control, but who collects the most crossfire.

A host is trying to manage how people come in. They are throttling the pace while making sure that people don't realize that that's what is happening. They are distracting an 8 PM reservation because a 5 PM walk-in decided an hour ago that they wanted to have a four-hour meal.

I asked a friend and former host what servers need to do to make their job easier. The response was simple: "Get them gone." If you can manage your tables well, and turn them regularly, it gives the hosts more options on where to shove the butts.

EXERCISES:

- **Stage.** You know the drill. Figure out what kind of reservation system your establishment uses. Understand how to seat people. Learn how to give great phone. You know less than you think you do, so listen to that perky marshmallow at the front desk.

- **Cookies. Coffee.** Again, the idea is to bribe these people... serve them. OH MY GOODNESS YOU WERE WAITING ON THE REST OF THE STAFF THE WHOLE TIME! Since these people are all doing things that help you make money, maybe you should be taking better care of them?

- **Restaurant floor plans.** Take a look at the various restaurant table layouts, and think about how many servers you might divide that floor into. Think about benefits for each section (close to the kitchen, close to a server station). The idea here is to try to understand specific patterns. Why do the hosts always seat a certain section first? How many people can you fit into a dinner service? What tables can be moved together in an emergency? If you can understand the floor's limits, you can help the host in an emergency.

- **Learn to be a better server.** Servers do their best work for the host when they can make grumpy people happy while getting customers in and out in a timely fashion. Repeat this mantra: "Happy and fast! Happy and fast!"

THE FUCKING CUSTOMER

One of my heroes is the late writer William Goldman. He was a grouchy curmudgeon perpetually pissed off by his own writing and by the movie business. The above is his legendary quote about the minds behind the Hollywood machine. His cynical philosophy goes double for restaurants, which shares a lot with showbiz.

In this chapter, we'll talk about the person walking in through the front door. We don't know them. They don't know us.

How should we approach these strangers?

What do you even call this total rando coming in for dinner? I've heard people refer to them as clients, customers, guests, humans, and assholes. There is value in discovering what best describes the people in your establishment.

Assholes and clients are about the same. I'd be just as happy serving them as not. The primary difference is that "clients" do their shady-shit off the premises. "Assholes" will punch and break things right in front of you.

Up to this point, I have referred to restaurant patrons as customers. That's the bare minimum. Every restaurant caters to customers. The customer relationship is purely transactional. These are people getting food as a function of lunch. They need service, but they don't want bells and whistles. They'd be as comfortable ordering from an iPad. This is a clean and straightforward relationship, and there's nothing wrong with it.

Everything you'd offer a customer you'd also extend to a guest or a human, but then you add to it. With a guest, you still keep an element of professional distance. They're a little like a Facebook friend who you only met once. You don't have their phone number and you don't want it.

Full human means treating them as a fully realized person. It's a relationship. It requires work and an investment of time. It's an investment you want to make with the right people.

When I go out, sometimes I'm a customer. Sometimes I want to be a guest. Sometimes I want the full human experience. I'd argue that labels aren't something the restaurant should put on people. Instead, it's something people give themselves. The person determines what they want to labeled. It's up to the restaurant to identify who is who and to understand that they serve different kinds of people in the same space.

At the same time, the best servers can turn almost any customer into a human. These servers make the person want to be seen that way. Humans are some of your most loyal repeat customers. They will come often, bring friends, recommend you to others, and tip generously.

The Lunacy of Restaurants
(1. The Ordinary World)

Restaurants are strange. Let's think about what's happening.

Pretend you're a customer. Let's say you're on a road trip. You get hungry, so you pick a building with a pleasing exterior and an "OPEN" sign in the window. You walk into this strange edifice. A person you've never met before greets you like an old friend. They give you some paper. You then read the paper and determine which collection of words will be the most delicious. No tasting. No examination of ingredients. Most of the time you don't even see a picture. You will likely never even see the people who created this menu or the people making it.

Another stranger approaches. They also treat you like a friend. Out of the blue, they tell you their name is Carl. You can ask Carl questions, but you don't know each other. Carl doesn't know that you have an unspeakably terrible fear of lamb, mint, and the word "rotisserie."

Carl doesn't make the food. Carl may barely know the menu. Carl doesn't usually work lunch. Carl doesn't even eat solid food. He lives off of protein powder.

But, you don't know any of this.

Carl tells you the burger is, "very popular" amongst the other random strangers who frequent this place. You order the burger. Why would Carl steer you wrong?

You eat the burger. God, it's awful. You don't have time. You choke it down.

It turns out that you're in a town famous for its lamb burgers. So famous that every burger served for 50 miles in every direction is made from lamb. As such no one even bothers writing "lamb" on the menu.

Who is to blame? Carl? The cook? The Chef? The town that enjoys lamb burgers? Is it your fault because your unspeakable fear comes from the fact that you cannot say the word "lamb?"

The check comes. You are expected to pay for your food and

all sorts of intangibles (water, sewage fees, rent, Chef's cocaine). A century of custom means you must now determine fair payment for the following: Carl, the busser, and the bartender who got ice from the basement then changed the carbonation tank and poured your soda.

Carl smiled. He answered your questions. He told you his name. That counts for something, right? Carl didn't make the burger or lie to you about its contents. He didn't lie about its popularity amongst the locals.

Do you leave 20%?

Carl is also a serial killer. But you don't know that.

The point is, what we experience as an average series of events is a flawed and awkward process. A big part of excellent service is untangling the problems inherent in this system.

People are Afraid, and They Have Baggage (2. Call To Adventure/ 3. Refusal Of The Call)

Hunger does strange things to people. In the beginning, I mentioned that this was a book about empathy. How do you feel when hungry? We all know how hungry children behave. Adults don't change. Instead, they get better at managing their responses to hunger. Sometimes.

When a customer is hungry, they're entering a restaurant to fix a problem. They are addressing pain. Again, it might be without conscious recognition, but they are "wounded." Their defenses are up.

Many customers and servers don't realize that the process of going into a restaurant can be subtly intimidating. Because we don't recognize it, some restaurants accidentally push people into putting up their defenses.

Restaurants take a certain amount of control away from people.

This can be as simple as the music level and the air temperature, but it's more than that. When people try a new restaurant or new cuisine, they are immediately off balance. Once a person is off balance, other fears creep in. Such as the fear of being taken advantage of. Depending on the person, that can be a huge hurdle to overcome.

A lot of people don't even realize that restaurants make them uncomfortable. They've been dealing with their issues for so long that they've come to accept restaurants as uncomfortable places. My grandmother was like this. She'd cultivated relationships at specific restaurants over decades. Because of this, anything outside those places was not to be trusted. Strange servers just wanted to take her money.

Also, food, like art, is subjective.

Take hummus. Some people have a specific reference point for what hummus is. Others have no reference for it at all. They may assume that all hummus tastes like the baba ganoush they tried twelve years ago (they don't know the difference). Or, if they hear it's made from chickpeas so they assume it tastes like something off the Wendy's Superbar circa 1989.

Even though you and the customer are using the same words, you might not be speaking the same language.

This is where the art of storytelling comes into play.

Telling Tales (4. Meeting The Mentor)

Being prepared for a certain amount of ignorance, unawareness, and defensiveness is important. Sometimes the best way to think about how to counter these problems is to think of yourself as a guide or a teacher. You are Yoda.

Early in my career, I worked at the Cheesecake Factory. It's a restaurant chain with an intensive training program. I had also just finished getting a literature degree. One day I realized that waiting on tables follows the twelve steps of Joseph Campbell's monomyth, also known as, "The Hero's Journey."

Campbell also happens to be the guy who inspired and informed Lucas' writing of the movie *Star Wars*.

The first steps of the monomyth:

1.) **The Ordinary World:** This is the Hero's (the customer's) reality.

2.) **Call To Adventure:** Hunger. It's a threat! Our hero must choose where to eat!

3.) **Refusal Of The Call:** In a hurry, she picks the closest place. Almost instantly she starts to question her choice: "The Hummus Barn." She's not sure what hummus is.

4.) **Meeting The Mentor:** You appear. The server is "the mentor," a person who will help guide the Hero. It starts by answering the question, "What's hummus?"

Here's the critical thing to remember: this is the diner's story. It's your job is to make them the hero. You do that by offering your expertise. The more you know about the restaurant and the food, the better mentor you'll be.

You are Obi-Wan, Yoda, and Gandalf. Remember, you have the power to turn a customer into a human.

Now that you're there to help, what comes next?

Your First Approach
(5. Crossing The Threshold)

Think about your favorite Mentors: Glinda the Good, Morpheus, or Mary Poppins. They offer advice and establish the Heroes' universe. Glinda explains Oz. Morpheus reveals the nature of the matrix. Mary Poppins lays down the rules. The first time you approach a table, you are establishing the rules and letting people in on the secret to a great meal. This interaction can make or break the whole experience.

If we assume that people might have some defenses up, do what you can to make your first "hello" a comfortable one. Don't come over too early and make them anxious, or so late they think you forgot about them. Judging that moment comes down to the little things.

Are they in a hurry? Or, are they waiting for more people? These are questions that can be easily answered if you're buddy-buddy with the host. Water is also an excellent opportunity to gauge a table. Water is a basic need, and it's usually free. You can place it down or pour it, and that's when you make a judgment based on their reaction to you. Do they acknowledge you with a smile, or duck and cover?

I usually offer a "hello" at this point, while giving them the option to ignore me. If I say anything else, it's usually something along the lines of, "Welcome. I'll be back in a minute, but is there anything I can get you right away?"

With this sentence, I've gently allowed them to order something. They can also volunteer information about their state of affairs. They can also stay quiet and shake their heads. I'm not pressuring them to say or do anything, but I'm also not refusing them the opportunity to do so. Based on their response I can get a basic idea of where their head's at. Then I set the pace.

Answering Questions
(6. Tests, Allies, Enemies)

It's important to assume that there are customers who don't know anything about your restaurant. No matter how popular or basic the place may be, someone out there doesn't get it. Over the years people have asked me to explain almost everything. There is also the problem of the know it all. The explosion of food television means that more people think they are experts. Often they don't know what in god's name they're talking about.

You have to be okay with all of this.

You have to understand how to correct and guide people with patient kindness. Some folks don't know that cheese is made with milk, or that the steak cannot be made with chicken.

Yes. These are real things that have happened.

Remember: the central problem is that if you act like people are stupid, they will think that *you* are stupid.

Are stupid?

This is also when you can set up alliances with the customers. Are there foods that they hate? Maybe you hate it too! Find out! Bond! Then once you have that rapport, you can talk about how the steak led you to divorce your terrible husband — Carl!

YES, THAT CARL! WE ALL HATE CARL!

If they don't know what hummus is, get them a tiny taste. Even if they don't order it, they have now tried it. You braved the wilderness of the kitchen, and brought them a bag of sand to prove that land exists! Words only go so far. Plus now you got them something FOR FREE! Leverage your relationship with the kitchen to help the customers understand the menu.

A nickel's worth of free hummus can take you a long way in this world. It shows that you are to be trusted. You and the table are now bonded!

The Waiting Game
(7. Approach To The Inmost Cave)

Waiting for food is hard. Keep beverages full. If you do bread service, bread them. Leave them be, but make yourself available.

This is the part where you need to be paying attention to things like ticket times. A lot of POS systems help you keep track of this.

At a basic level, you should also know the expected time it takes for a dish to leave the kitchen. If the steak takes 15 minutes, but everything else in the order is ready in 10. Know how to navigate that. Are they in a hurry? People will give you leeway if you can explain what's happening. It's not knowing what's going on that makes people anxious.

Many factors will affect the speed of food. Sometimes having Joey working the grill will change the ticket times. If you have friends in the kitchen, they can educate you. They'll fill you in on Joey's nickname: "Slowy."

Always remember, sometimes a simple distraction can make a table forget something is taking a long time. Sometimes it's a joke, a fly-by, or dropping off an origami animal with no explanation.

If the ticket time is taking forever, check in with a manager. The manager is your Gandalf. They can provide more distractions, a surprise snack, or they can talk to the Chef that scares you.

This is the point in the meal when you give your heroes the specialized tools they'll need to complete their quest. Maybe this is a soup or serving spoon. It could be share plates, condiments, or a tiny baggie of MSG designed to look like an eight-ball of yayo.

What are the items that will allow them to enjoy their meal more?

The Food Arrives (8. Ordeal)

This is the part of the meal where everything can go to shit, and fast. It also the point that allows you to be the hero.

Is something missing from the order? Is something not cooked right? Was one of the items not what they thought it was? Did you make a mistake or mishear an order?

If I'm not dropping off the food, I make sure to walk past the table as the food comes to rest, or shortly after. I don't need to interact. Besides, people HATE it when you ask how everything is when that first bite of food is in their mouth.

I'm not there to interfere, but I want to make sure that I'm nearby and available. I always think of my addiction to ketchup. Whatever comes in a ramekin is never enough. If I don't see a ketchup bottle on the table, sometimes I order my burger with, "extra ketchup," but not always. In a burger/fries situation, the standard "side" is never enough.

I can only eat fries bathed in a slaughter of ketchup. The fries will go cold before I eat them naked, and cold fries are like eating playdough.

People like their food the way they like their food. The restaurant may think they know the best way to enjoy a dish, but sometimes they're wrong. It's up to the server to make sure that no fries go cold.

The Beasts are Slain (9. Reward)

When the plates are nearing empty, it can feel like the job is over. This is not always the case. This is the part where those who know what they are doing can turn a customer into a human.

This is the time for the little things. You checked in, and they loved a dish. Can you get them a recipe? Are they the kind of diners who would flip over meeting the Chef? Can you get them an extra side of something even they didn't realize they wanted? Is there a "special" off-the-menu fry-sauce?

Once they are done, start clearing the plates. Take as much off as you can, while being aware that there are a variety of standards. Some people swear up and down that it's rude to clear the table while others are still eating. Other people are like, "WHY IS THIS STILL IN MY WAY?"

In traditional service, there are established codes. In particular, crossed silverware on your plate is supposed to mean you're finished. I've never worked in a place where that was a universally effective sign.

As such, I always look for the "plate-pop" which is one of those things that once you notice, is hard to un-notice. People reflexively, almost always, push their plate forward when they are done. Sometimes it's tiny, barely a centimeter. I see it at home. I see it at work. I can't explain it, and I also catch myself doing it without thinking.

In short: Be aware. Clean up. Tie-up loose ends. This is where people start feeling accomplished. In reality, we're getting them ready for what's to come. I was trained with the adage, "You clean the table so that they forget they ate. That way they order dessert."

Dinner: The Sequel (10. The Road Back)

The doggie bag was a big deal in France when they started to offer it... in 2018. In the United States, it's always been a part of the meal's value. You get obscene sized portions. Because of that, you can enjoy some now and some later.

I always offer to wrap up food, but I also understand people who like to do it themselves. When I go out, I enjoying packing up my food. Because I want to keep certain things separate, and I want all the sauce, and I am anal retentive. I give people the option. If they ask for boxes, I make it my job to know if they are asking to "be polite" or if they want to do it themselves. I can't tell you how to make that call.

Once I asked a guy if he wanted me to wrap up the other half of his tuna salad sandwich. He immediately lifted the drippy half sandwich off the plate and shoved it into my hands. His dining companion laughed, but I didn't flinch. I took the sandwich to the back and wrapped it up. I then scrubbed thrice and returned it.

I not stupid.

This is also where you can excel. Did they want to pack up dip, but ate all the chips? Get a few more for the to-go (if your restaurant is comfortable with that).

I have worked at a few "shared plates" restaurants. I will sometimes reassure tables by saying something like, "If you're worried about ordering too much, I'm happy to pack up anything as you go along. For example, the corn you ordered is excellent the next day." Then, when the corn comes four courses later, they're ready to have me pack it up almost immediately. This way they still have room for the next two courses.

It's Not Just Desert (11. Resurrection)

It pays to leave room for dessert, but we'll talk more about that in the next chapter. If they're feeling full, maybe they'd prefer to drink their dessert. I worked with a server who constantly pushed espresso martinis. They cost twice as much as any desert, and even if people feel like they don't have room for food, they may have room for a drink. If you don't know about Amari, look it up. I'm sometimes shocked at how effective a shot of Amaro Sibilla (my favorite) is at making a person feel like they still have room.

Never force desert. This is the ultimate suggestive sell. I don't want my human's drunk, and I don't want them stuffed. I want them satisfied and (mostly) sober.

But, leaving people with a sweet taste in their mouths is good business. One of the most powerful tools can be the "tiny dessert." A cookie. A small scoop of ice cream. Nothing elaborate, just something sweet. Depending on the establishment, maybe you can suggest the Chef have an off-menu "dollar dessert."

GTFO (12. Return With The Elixir)

There comes a point when people need to go. The table is clean. You've dropped the check. You've left them a thank you note. You tell them you can't wait to see them again. Be genuine, but firm. You now have a friend for life.

But remember, you need to make more friends.

This is the point where you make sure they are so happy that they can't wait to tell everyone about the place. As the hero, this is where they deliver "fire" to the people. They leave, and they will write a Yelp review. Make sure they write a good one.

Here are some things to think about. I have their check on me before they order dessert. I want them to order dessert, but if they're going to go, I want them to feel free to leave. If they snap their fingers for the check, I am the genii granting their wish.

You have to be able to read your tables.

Some will be offended if you instantly drop the check. The spell will be broken. If this is the case, walk around the corner and come back with the check. With other people, I pull out my book, and I drop it. They want out. They don't need the illusion. At the end of the day, I am not a genii, and they are not heroes because they ate $200 worth of food.

Now you know how to build a story. But just because you have a pattern to follow, don't just fall into mindless repetition. Don't be Hollywood and keep rebooting and recycling shit.

There are variations, and most of the useful variations come down to learning science...

EXERCISES:

- **Go to Quora.com.** Read the responses to the following question: "What irritates you the most about servers?" Then, find all the other questions and answers about serving and restaurants. Taking criticism is hard. This way you can see all the shit that bugs people about "other" servers. It's always enlightening to learn from others' failures. Again, there are many questionable experts here, so beware of bullshit.

- **Watch more YouTube.** If you like words or movies, watch an interview with William Goldman. Produced by the Writers Guild Foundation, it's called "The Writer Speaks: William Goldman." It's entertaining, and any service employee would benefit by learning how to tell a good story.

- **Watch *Star Wars*.** You already made it to chapter four of a potentially very dull book. Reward yourself. I'm sure it has some relevance. The lasting effects of blue milk?

- **Watch *Waiting, Babbett's Feast* and *Le Grand Bouffet*.** The first of these films is humorous and a bit dated. The second one is romantic and timeless. The third is disturbing and disgusting. All three films have their moments, and they are all about people's relationships with food. They also use story architecture to tell three completely different stories. I recomend watching *Babbett* last to leave a pleasant taste in your mouth. This may be the only point in history where someone recommends watching these three movies together.

FUCKING FINESSE
AND SALES SKILLS

Any server should read M.F.K. Fisher's *Define this Word*; it's a tale of perfect service gone awry.

This server with "butter-colored hair" and an "odd pale voluptuous mouth," read Fisher like a book. She catered to her. She left an impression. Unfortunately, she also bludgeoned Fisher to death with her service.

Sometimes, "fantastic service" fails.

At this point, you know everything about your restaurant. You know the food. You know your team. You know the story you're trying to tell the customer.

Now it's a matter of finesse. It can be easy to default into "smiles and hugs." This means acting happy in the hope that people will have a good time. Don't do that. I hate smiles and hugs, and so do a lot of people. This approach is like an absentee parent who buys extravagant gifts for a child. It's an artificial substitute for empathy.

In your day to day routine, balls-out sincerity isn't always necessitated. Many (if not most) of your interactions are transactional. This leads us into another component of service that's important to balance — Sales.

Sales are what keeps the lights on, but an unchecked sales motive turns good service into a TV dinner with the commercials turned all the way up.

Sincerity, empathy, and sales: these are an essential and delicate balance. What follows are some tips and tricks. But don't incorporate them into your job blindly. Think about how you use this information.

It's like baking cookies. You have the list of ingredients, but now you need to combine them in the right way. There is an order of operations and a technique to follow. There are always ways to change the recipe to suit your needs.

To give you an idea of what you're juggling, let's make a batch of chocolate chip cookies.

STEP ONE: Creaming

> 1/2 cup butter (1 stick or 4 ounces)
> 1/3 cup + 1 tablespoon granulated sugar (5.73 ounces)
> 1/3 cup brown sugar, light or dark, packed (2.5 ounces)

When making cookies, you start by creaming together cool (just below room temperature) butter and sugar. This builds the structure. Mixing the butter and sugar like this creates a latticework of fat and sugar around tiny air bubbles. If the butter is too hot (or melted) you don't get the same bubbles, which results in a denser and chewier cookie. It's not bad; it's different. Stella Parks (@BraveTart) has a fantastic breakdown of the science at

Serious Eats, in an article titled, "Cookie Science: Why Cream Butter and Sugar?"

White sugar is sweet but lacks character. But, white sugar also creates bigger and more beautiful air bubbles. Brown sugar (white sugar with molasses added to it) has a unique and complex depth of flavor. It also has acid, a chemical component which will be important later. Brown sugar also adds more chew, while white sugar adds more crunch, to the final product.

What we've discussed in this book so far is structural. Once that stuff understood, you add finesse. This is the stuff that augments the basics. This is the part where you choose the temperature of your butter and how dark your brown sugar will be.

"The customer is always right," and the "No" that sounds like a "Yes."

Santa Claus. At some point, children learn the truth. The service industry has its version of this lie: "The customer is always right." Santa instills children with a sense of wonder while imposing behavioral blackmail. It's a morality shortcut. Be good or else. Likewise, servers are fed a line to make sure that they default to taking care of the customer.

But someday this server will wait on a terrible person. Awful human beings abound. That's when they find out that Santa's a lie and Krampus is coming for dinner. Some servers can brush it off, but others aren't sure how to balance this against what they've been told.

This saying needs to die. Sometimes it succeeds, but it does so at a cost. When it fails, it instills a terrible attitude in people. The customer should be heard, and every reasonable attempt to understand them should be made. But no, they aren't always right.

Alas, the myth persists.

Even if we know the truth, how do you deal with customers who still believe in Santa Claus?

You learn how to make your "no" sound like "yes."

Sometimes the customer will ask for something you can't do. This could be ordering an item that your restaurant doesn't make. It might be a request that's not possible.

Make an earnest effort to understand the request. Suppose the customer says, "I'm allergic to carbohydrates, can you make this dish with caviar instead of pasta?" This is a nonsense request. But, listen to what is being said and take it at face value.

An "allergy" to carbohydrates (as opposed to gluten) sounds like bullshit. But that is the customer's stated core concern. Take it in. At this point, the absurdity of asking for a pile of caviar topped with pasta sauce is not the issue. My first response would be to request clarity and see if I couldn't offer a more reasonable alternative. "Sir, I'll happily ask about the caviar, but something I know for certain she can do is put the pasta sauce on the steak. Would that work?"

This is where knowing the menu, and having a broad idea of how things are prepared will come in handy.

Asking this question also gives me a gauge on their sanity/flexibility. If I'm pretty sure we can't accommodate the request, I have mentally prepared the requestor for other possibilities. No matter if he says "Yes" or "No," I can now take the next step.

I will always "double check" a request, even on things that I know the kitchen won't do. Sometimes I mean those quotation marks and sometimes I don't. There are times when I walk into the kitchen and ask the chef where he bought his pepper mill. Then I walk out and tell them, "I am so sorry, we don't have enough caviar right now. I can offer you the steak with a side of pasta sauce, and a smaller side of caviar."

If I can help the kitchen by saying "no," and still please the customer, that is what I will do.

But sometimes this is a puzzle the server and the kitchen can figure out together. Good chefs I've worked with have enjoyed problem-solving on behalf of the guest. That is... when they are not brown-eye deep in the weeds.

I once had a table with a woman who wanted a fish entree to eat with her dining companions, who had all ordered steaks. We didn't have a fish entree. The closest was a small octopus appetizer. I talked to her and listened to her requirements. Then I went to the chef and asked if they could put two octopus appetizers on the same plate along with a small side salad. I rung it up as a single entree, but she paid for two octopus appetizers and a side salad. She loved it, and the problem wasn't hard to solve.

I didn't say yes to her request, but I also didn't say no. Instead, I listened and figured out how to make *something* work.

The Art of the Apology

Danny Meyer has a lecture called, "The Irrelevancy of Being Right." Yes, that's the wrong word. That's the point. Check out the talk, but the general idea is that some customers don't understand what they're asking for. The important thing is not to correct them or try to figure out who is correct. The important thing is to find the point they're reaching for and figure out how to get them there.

Part of that is knowing when and how to negotiate with the kitchen. Sometimes you can't get them what they want, and that's when you need to know how to apologize.

Of course, an apology is useful not only when a customer is wrong, but for our shortcomings. "I'm so sorry..." was one of the first valuable phrases I remembered learning in the restaurant business. At first, I used it too much. When you do that, there comes the point where it becomes cloying and insincere. The key comes not in apologizing reflexively, but in being aware when you say it. Being able to apologize with sincerity is essential. But to do it, you have to be paying attention. There's also more to an apology. You need to find out if you can fix the situation.

Sometimes there's nothing you can do. The wine is spilled. You wiped the table, cleaned them up, poured them another glass, and offered to pay for the dry cleaning.

The Arizona State University W.P. Carey School of Business ran what they called "The 2017 Customer Rage Study." In it, they discovered, "When companies offered a free remedy, such as an apology, only 23 percent of people were happy. Satisfaction jumped to 73 percent when they received monetary relief and free remedies such as an apology."

Sometimes an apology is best served with a free dessert.

Follow the Rules(ish)

There are certain standards of etiquette expected in restaurants of a certain level. Any restaurant, no matter the level, benefits from being aware of these rules. But there should be a discussion of what's practical.

Below are some basic "rules" I've found listed in various places. Some of these apply to specific restaurants. Many of them are ignored in the majority of casual eateries.

- Proper posture: no slouching, never cross your arms, never put hands in your pockets.
- Do not engage in informal conversations with guests or staff on the floor.
- Only hold wine glasses by the stem.
- Use a cloth napkin when pouring wine to wipe drips from the mouth of the bottle.

- Serve food from a platter from the diner's left.
- Serve a plated and composed dish from the diner's right.
- Serve, pour and refill drinks from the right.
- Clear food from the diner's left.
- When someone leaves the table, fold their napkin, and place it back neatly at their seat.
- Don't auction (call out) entrées when food is delivered.
- The guest to the host's right is served first (usually a woman).
- Ladies are always served first.
- Dishes are served around the table continuing to the right.
- Plates should be rotated when being served, so the protein of a dish is facing the guest, or whatever position the chef dictates (aka "Best Bite Forward").
- Completely clear and prep the table between each course.
- Never clear plates while someone is still eating.
- Never let diners feel like you want them to leave.
- Don't make your diners ask for the check. Bring it promptly.

Most practical managers believe the customer's needs should supersede etiquette. There are so many gray areas here that can get you into trouble. I can think of a dozen reasons why "serve drinks from the right" shouldn't be a universal default. A more obvious rule that can screw you? "With mixed gender couples, serve ladies first."

Read your table, and discuss the finer points with your team.

Gender Identity

Speaking of gender and proper service, let's talk about it. It's inevitable that someone believes that addressing "gender identity" doesn't belong in a guide to service. They might say that acknowledging or discussing gender identity isn't part of the job. They might say that recognizing people's gender identity isn't about treating people fairly. They might argue that it's about giving certain people "special treatment."

If you read that last sentence unironically, you are in the wrong fucking business.

Being conscientious about things like gender (and race) is important. I say this as a person with a hearty serving of privilege. I have it easy when I go out. People see me and recognize me in the same way that I perceive myself. If I go out with three other guys and a gal, no one asks, "How are you, ladies?"

In the service industry, our job is to let people feel comfortable, validated, and happy enough to spend their money. At a basic level, this means recognizing people as they perceive themselves.

Empathy, warmth, and respect go a long way towards making people happy. I recommend using gender-neutral terms when talking to a table for the first time. Don't box people in, and let them dictate how they want to be recognized. Assume nothing, and watch how people react.

I once asked a table, "Can I do anything more for you ladies?" At which point one of them, masculine in their presentation, said, "Who are you calling a lady?"

I fucked up. Intentionally or no, I made this person feel excluded and ignored. That's not empathy. After this incident, I tried to be more aware. I practiced, and I worked to make gender-neutral terms my conversational norm.

Gender neutral terms may not work at every table, but try to use them as much and as often as possible. Be aware that words like "dude" and "folks" should be used sparingly. These are the truffle oil of gender-neutral service. Sometimes it works, but usually, it comes across as artificial and clumsy.

It may seem like an annoyance to you, but for your guests, it's their whole identity. Take the time to recognize people as they want to be recognized.

Fuck Racial Stereotypes

Just forget them. I've worked in so many restaurants where someone will list out an ethnic group, how they behave, what food they order, and how they tip. I have been guilty of it, and it's something I regret.

That said, many stereotypes appear to hold. I'm a fat white guy who loves mac and cheese, mashed potatoes, and pork. Sounds about right. Although, sometimes I also eat vegan soul food. Let the person dictate what they need and want, and respect each request as it comes. Recognize your biases enough to work through them. At the end of the shift, it does you less good, and more potential harm, to make assumptions.

There's a good chance you don't know people as well as you think you do.

Keep reminding yourself that these people are strangers and you don't know their story. Get to know them. Genuine interest will give you real insight. Think of all the times in your life when someone assumed something about you. How often was that assumption a good thing?

There's also a big difference between anticipating and assuming.

What's that difference?

Write Your Script

Assuming means, you're basing your actions on externals (race, gender, clothes). Anticipation means you're addressing what people in your restaurant regularly need.

Write down what questions you get in an average shift. Think about how often people ask for napkins with a specific dish. Are your tables always short on water? Why? Consider these events. Then put together some standard answers and actions and write your script.

We've established that it's easier to do things ahead of time. You know your team, you know your tea box, and you know your menu. Now work on the perfect comeback. Do you know how you think of the ideal comeback the next day? Next time that happens at work write it down and be ready for the next time.

There's a good chance there will be a next time. This is a job where you often say the same things day after day. It pays to have "canned" responses. These can be jokes, one-liners, or phrases of reassurance. The automatic nature of these responses should never appear canned.

Instead, they should make it seem that you're a genius.

If you've ever asked a table, "Can I get you anything else?" you've inevitably heard, "How about a million bucks?" Have a response for this shitty joke. It'll prevent your face from collapsing into a death glare. Without missing a beat say, "Me first."

See? It doesn't even have to be that good! But knowing what question is coming, and having a fast, smart-ass response can win over a table.

Then there are the questions, "What do you recommend?" or, "Is such-n-such dish any good?"

Sometimes there is an easy answer to this question. But at a good restaurant, pretty much everything should fall on the list. That means that it will come down to personal preference, there will be dishes you like that others hate. There will also be dishes you hate that are super popular.

I struggled to find the right answers to these questions. My friend Victor came up with a proper response. "There's only one thing on the menu I'm not crazy about. If you pick it, I'll let you know."

This answer gives you leeway. If they want, they can make it a game, but usually, they smile and dive into the menu. This answer provides them the freedom to pick whatever they want to select. It also means that if something is truly not good, you've given yourself an out.

This kind of vagueness may seem unnecessary, but it makes it easier for you to appear consistent. Being consistent in your words and actions throughout the meal is essential. This may seem like a little thing, but remember you are a stranger. As a stranger, there is a natural subconscious drive not to trust you. Thinking about what you say, and how you say it — consistency — will also make you appear more trustworthy.

Back to building your cookies...

STEP TWO: Wet Ingredients

> 1 large egg
> 1 teaspoon vanilla

Mix the wet ingredients. Add them slowly to your creamed butter and sugar so that they incorporate fully.

The egg gives the cookie substance. The white helps with structure. The fatty yolk increases the cookie's tenderness, taste, and richness — more egg results in a chewier cookie. The vanilla adds a depth of flavor and highlights the complexities in the brown sugar.

Without this step, you're headed towards a simple piece of shortbread. But with it, you're on the path to a melty and delicious sugar cushion of a cookie. Reflecting on the last chapter, this is the part where we soften and tenderize a customer into a human.

Identify what kind of person you're dealing with.

One of the things to keep in mind in a restaurant is that excellent service is about making someone feel heard.

Let's revisit the question, "What would you recommend?" I currently work in a restaurant that specializes in "global cuisine." This means there's a little bit of everything on the menu. In this instance, I almost always ask them, "If you were home ordering delivery, what would you get? Pizza, BBQ, Chinese food?" Other variations on this question are, "What's your other favorite restaurant?" or "What's your favorite dish to cook?"

I've asked these questions for years because talking food works for me. But, there's also a principle behind it. It's a principle expressed in the book, *Never Split the Difference* by FBI negotiator Chris Voss. He talks about how when you're negotiating you need to, "know what their religion is." In other words, "What is their measuring stick?" If you're going to give someone a useful recommendation, you have to know what their standards are.

This is also something that demonstrates that you're listening to them. It allows you to tell someone that a dish (with similarities to one they already like) is good. In other words, you're telling someone, that a "good dish" is "good" because it has things in it that they told you were "good."

Extroverts and Introverts

You can usually tell someone's demeanor by looking them in the eyes. Where do their eyes go? Is it a steady stare? Are they looking down at the table? How do they speak? Extroverts tend to respond quickly and think out loud. Introverts tend to be quieter and consider their answers.

Identify where someone falls on this spectrum, and identify where you fall as well. If you are an extrovert (there's a good chance that you are), make space for introverts to find answers. Extroverts may tend to click with other extroverts, but sometimes there can be a butting of heads. If you're introverted, learn how to deal with extroverts. This might mean learning how to cut them off politely, or managing how much you listen to them.

Again, I recommend the book *Never Split the Difference*. In many ways, a server at a table is a negotiation, and the book has many helpful strategies for that situation.

When dealing with assertive people, being silent tends to indicate to them that they should keep talking. Sometimes you'll need to cut these people off, or you won't get anywhere. Don't think of it as rude. Think of it as directing the conversation.

A person that tends towards accommodation tends to go silent when upset or angry. If these people hate the food, it will be up to you to read them and figure out what they need. If you can listen to them, and make them feel at ease, you are more likely to coax information from them. For these people, the simple act of telling you the problem may prevent them from directing hate via Yelp.

For analytical people, if they're silent, that may not be a bad thing. It means they're considering the situation.

There is so much out there about how to read people. *Never Split the Difference*, is an excellent start. Old issues of *Psychology Today* at the library can open your eyes to the basics of human behavior. Even taking the time to understand Maslow's Hierarchy of Needs will teach you volumes.

If you want to get deep into this stuff, learn about a tool of performance psychics and magicians called, "Cold Reading." There are books and courses and learning it is worth it for the potential party tricks alone.

Shoes

I worked with Simon. Simon was obsessed with sneakers and fancy watches. Simon was a salesman. He used to sell cars but realized he could make as much, and have more flexibility, selling wine. For Simon, it was about sizing people up by their watches and shoes.

Watches are less universal these days, but almost every restaurant still requires shoes.

I've been told many times that judging shoes are the way to go. I don't put much stock in it. It seems that most people wear shoes that reflect other more obvious personality indicators. But Simon was a good salesman, so I can't dismiss it.

Here's a crib sheet I unearthed on how to judge people by their shoes:

- Pricey shoes go with high income. Watch for women wearing red-soled Louboutins, or learn to recognize high-end sneakers. This feels sexist, but I'm told servers should pay particular attention to men in expensive shoes. Statistics show that men leave higher tips, and are often the ones picking up the check.

- Showy and brightly colored shoes tend to belong to extroverts.

- Conscientious people wear shoes that are not new but have been well cared for. Consider each table approach and take along a calm demeanor.

- Agreeable people tend to wear practical and functional shoes. Suggestive selling is your best bet.

- Ankle boots are the choice of aggressive folks. They might respond well to aggressive sales techniques. Prepare for bluntness.

- Calm personalities choose to wear uncomfortable looking shoes.

- Those who lean left on the political spectrum tend to wear 'shabbier and less expensive' shoes. Conservative tend the other way.

- Dull and boring shoes tend to belong to 'aloof and repressive' characters. These are functional folks. Treat the table as no-nonsense. Basics only.

- New shoes that still showed signs of extreme polishing indicated relationship "attachment anxiety." Include all the sauces with their to-go leftovers.

While some find these reliable indicators, I find that most of these tells come through in other ways. It's in their entire outfit, how they present themselves, and how they talk to you.

Browse the Relevant Pop Culture

No one has to be an expert on food to be a server, but it helps. But, more than being an expert, being aware of pop culture food trends can be handy. Glance through the food TV channels. See what they're making on YouTube. Even a quick look at your local alternative weekly food section will gain you insight. It's best to check on a source that's relevant to your restaurant's demographic.

For example: If your customers are Martha Stewart apostles, check in with Marty's rag *Living*.

Even if you learn every tip for decoding a person, most of the time it's still a gut response. If you live in a city, and you interact with people regularly, you have developed most of these skills already.

On to the next step in your cookie.

STEP THREE: Dry Ingredients

1/2 teaspoon salt
1/4 teaspoon baking soda
1/2 teaspoon baking powder
1 1/2 cups All-Purpose Flour

Salt is a flavor enhancer. At lower concentrations it curbs bitterness. It also boosts sweetness, sour, and that elusive flavor known as umami. Baking soda is a chemical leavener that adds "air" to the cookie. One of the things that activate it is the acid in the molasses of brown sugar. Baking powder is baking soda that's been bound to an inert acid. It then activates with moisture. Or with "double acting" baking powder, once with moisture and once with heat. Both these leaveners enhance the bubbles you made in the creaming process. Why add both? Too much powder can add a bitter flavor. Too much soda can add a soapy taste. Adding both powder and soda makes for a thicker, lighter, better tasting, cookie. Sifting or whisking these dry ingredients, and combining them in batches, also makes for a more uniform final product.

This is the part that we think of as the "meat" of the cookie. This is the substance. The rest is tasty, but without this part, you're just scarfing down a sweet, sweaty gob of fat and salmonella.

Now we're talking about the "meat" of your job. Sales. In many ways, this is your "real" job.

Servers are preaching to the choir. Hungry people will order food no matter who takes their order. But sales are not only about making money. Proper sales technique help you build a restaurant's clientele. It's your point of strategic value in the restaurant system.

Customer service exists to support sales. There is no customer service without it. The bill is how a restaurant continues to exist. The bare economics of it all used to make me uneasy, and it's one reason I got involved in volunteering in my off hours. I concluded that if the job is about empathy, that means helping people make good purchases. We help them make their own best choices. In turn, they reward us with their business.

There is a slippery element to sales and many intangible elements. Even as I offer advice and techniques, a lot of it is less concrete. Don't be fooled. Companies follow these same rules to sell everything from toilet paper to automobiles. While some of this seems like baseball superstition, we're actually talking about "server-sabermetrics."

Mirroring

If there's a magic spell in service, it's the psychological principle known as mirroring. It shows up in books on negotiation (including *Never Split the Difference*), books on dating, and in everything I've ever read on sales.

The idea is so simple it seems silly, but it's useful. Watch your table. Be aware of things like speech cadence, breathing patterns, and body language. Do as they do. Mirroring appears to increase empathy by subconsciously communicating similar interests or beliefs. Be careful not to drift into blunt imitation. Playing copy-cat with a stranger will only make you look insane.

If they like something, talk about how you like it. If they dislike something, frown, and return their same level of concern. If they seem distant and quiet, give them distance and talk low.

The Sullivan Nod

The story is that this technique is named after a restaurant consultant named Jim Sullivan. This is a strategy for when you have to present a list of options. The idea is that you smile and nod at the item on the list that you want the "mark" to bite at. Are you listing off the available liquors? Nod when you mention the top shelf.

Does this work? Maybe! No one has hard proof, but it's so universally accepted as gospel, you might as well give it a shot.

Foreshadowing and Familiarity

Mentioning a dessert option at the beginning of the meal will prepare them for it later. Bringing attention to any item will make it harder to ignore. This is the beauty of specials, but any dish on the menu you bring attention to will become more appealing. It plays on the psychological principle of "familiarity." Mere repetition makes people feel like they are more familiar with the dish. It can give the dish an aura of popularity, even if this is the first night it's on the menu.

People like things they are familiar with. Being exposed to something repeatedly makes it more attractive.

People also respond to consensus. Letting people know that, "Everyone loves this" or that this is "the most popular dish" will sell them. I recommend being accurate with this kind of declaration, remember, it pays to be consistent. But, there can be an aspect of this for nearly every dish. "This is the Chef's favorite!" or, "The bar manager orders this every night for dinner!"

In marketing, they call this "social proof." This is the idea that people are more likely to do something if someone else is doing it. People have a hard time being the first, but they also don't want to be left behind.

"The chef recommends…"

Some people command a natural sense of authority. I've been told that sometimes strangers feel this way about me. I believe I'm good at selling food because people will accept food advice from a fat man. If you don't have the gift of girth, use the above phrase. The Chef is the highest authority on food in the restaurant. As such their recommendation carries the most weight.

While this may seem like a no brainer, consider how you use this tactic. I'd recommend against just spouting the familiar phrase. Instead opt for a genuine conversation with your chef about what they enjoy, and why they love it. Find a way to enter these facts into conversation naturally.

Presume the "Yes"

If your selling oysters to a table, asking, "Starting off with a dozen or a half-dozen oysters tonight?" is more likely to sell some oysters than, "Would you like some oysters?" The first presents the order as a given, with details to be determined. The table may only order one oyster, but at least that's a sale. A general question that requires a "yes" or "no" is less encouraging. This approach can be perceived as pushy. Some tables will appreciate this approach. There are also tables that will immediately identify you as an asshole. Read. Your. Table.

There are sneaky ways to use this too. This doesn't work everywhere, and it can backfire if the table isn't paying attention. When you confirm their order, include all dishes discussed but not necessarily ordered. They will either correct you or look at each other and say, "Oh, why not."

The Principle of Reciprocity

Restaurants are built on the Principle of Reciprocity. Eating makes people happy. It surges endorphins. Given this, people will tend to give back what they feel that they owe. If you provide a great meal with excellent service, this effect should be generated naturally. The classic example of harnessing this principle is the belief that people leave a higher tip if mints or candies land with the check. They got a free treat, so they feel subconsciously obligated to return the favor.

You can use it in smaller, subtler, ways as well. When someone says, "Thank you!" responses like, "You'd do the same for me," or "No problem! I appreciate you asking!" invoke a feeling of being part of the solution. You're confirming that they are a positive force. This then generates more positive emotions.

The "Backfire Effect" and "The Outsiders"

If you know your table, telling them directly and enthusiasticly what they should order will work every time. But if you haven't built that relationship, one of the worst things you can do is tell someone point blank what they need to do or buy.

Being direct, when you don't know the customer, can lead to something known as the "Backfire Effect." People will double down on rejection when presented with views that oppose their beliefs. If you tell them they have to try the fish, and they hate fish, you are now not to be trusted. It then becomes harder for you to sell them anything else.

Then there is the prospect of identifying "outsiders." I generally dislike this technique (though useful) because it's ruined civil discourse. This is where you recognize an outgroup, and in doing so, you bring people with similar thinking to your side. Things as simple as chastising fans of an opposing sports team can deliver a table to your way of thinking. I'm amazed at how effective it can be.

This can be silly: "You don't like carrots? Me neither!" Now you can effectively sell them all the carrot free dishes. They identify you as one of them. As a born and bred New Englander, when I lived in LA, it was easy for me to sell every Red Sox fan at least two rounds of drinks. This technique is insidious and easy to manipulate.

"You don't like those people? Hey! I don't like those people either!"

This technique can sell sodas and ruin civilizations.

Upselling

This isn't a psychological principle, and in many ways, this is the easiest thing to add into your routine today. It's simple, and it helps. This is just about knowing what's available, and being able to offer things reflexively.

Know your premium liquors so you can tack on an additional $2-$3 for every round of drinks. Know that a hamburger is better with bacon and cheese (another $2-$3). Know the differences between the $40 Chardonnay and the $60 Chardonnay.

These can seem like paltry sums, but remember *Office Space*? Grab enough partial pennies off the table, and soon you'll be burning down Initech.

STEP FOUR: Chunks, Chips, Nuts, and Raisins

> 2 cups chocolate chips (any variety), nuts, raisins, and/or other dried fruit. (Optional or assorted)

Preheat the oven to 375°F and line a couple of sheet pans with parchment paper. Fold the above chunks, chips, nuts, and raisins into your batter. Scoop the batter out by the tablespoon onto the prepared baking sheets. Space them about 2" apart. Bake the cookies for about 12 minutes. Since ovens can vary, go until a.) they smell "right" b.) They're golden brown with a touch of darkness around the edges. If you bake them short, they'll be a bit softer and the longer you go, the harder they'll be. (Dirrrty).

This is where you make the cookie your own. This is not structural; it's all your flair. The following suggestions add flavor and character to your service. They're also primarily dictated by the mix of your personality and the restaurant's brand.

Specials

I've always thought I was good as selling food because I was fat. There is a small part of me that thinks people believe they're "winning" by taking food away from a fat man. But I've no proof of this. What I do have evidence of is I have a knack for selling specials.

There are restaurants where specials are an attempt to move stuff that was going bad. Often specials are the Chef's attempt to try something new. It's a chance to use a rare ingredient, or it's a test run for something that might go on the menu later. These are things that get me excited, and it's easy for me to talk about.

What follows is personal and anecdotal; I have no science to back it up. In popular, high-end, restaurants it's easier to sell specials and push specific items early in the evening. I have a spitball theory. People who take early reservations at these restaurants took them for a reason. Often, they really wanted to eat there and these early times were the best they could do. They want to be at THAT restaurant. If the chef at that special place is running something special, they are more likely to opt-in on it.

Whether this is true or not, as a waiter adopting this POV is to your advantage. It forces you to mention the specials right away. The more you talk about the specials, the more it forces you to figure out how to talk about them.

You can practice the process of "specialing." Pick an item from the menu, and talk about it, not as a special, but as a "featured item." Say something like, "If you want to try something different, you should think about the razor clams. There aren't many restaurants in the area carrying them, and it sets us apart."

This leads to the next idea: scarcity. FOMO. Some restaurants are particular that they don't want people to sell this way. That should be respected. When it's true, it's a great way to get people on board. "We only have a couple left, but I can put it on hold if you're interested," works nearly every time.

If scarcity isn't something you can use, there's also "priming." This technique can be used in almost any context and is largely subjective. Priming involves applying appealing words to certain dishes. Say there's a customer who looks like they're celebrating. Using terms like "luxurious" or "special occasion" as you recommend the caviar makes a direct association.

A corollary to this is to focus on value, not price. The most important thing to talk about is what's great on the menu, not the most expensive. Find the exclusive item, the things that you can only get there. Focus on the pleasure of a dish. That's value.

It's also helpful to be presumptive. In *The Art of War*, Sun Tzu says, "Every battle is won or lost before it's ever fought." This is true of dinner specials as much as anything else. If you can figure out what excites you about a dish and why you would buy it, you can sell it.

Lies

Speaking of Sun Tzu:

> *"All warfare is based on deception. Hence when able to attack we must seem unable. When using our forces we must seem inactive. When we are near we make the enemy believe we are far away. When far away we must make the enemy believe we are near."*

Deception in a restaurant works on several levels. There is the fundamental illusion that a restaurant is, "a party with friends." There is the illusion that everything is made at the moment. But there are also lies service personnel use to help things run smoothly.

I've thought a lot about this. In a lot of ways, this is something that is easily misconstrued and is a reason why some customers hate eating out. Lying to customers is both a great tool and also will leave you high and dry if you use it too much or get caught. It's not something to take lightly.

Sometimes the lie is small and positive. I have lied about getting the "whole tip" in a pooled house. This way a table feels good about rewarding me with an exorbitant tip. Then there are grey areas. You might say a dish was, "refired for quality" when a dish was actually left off a ticket. This is a lie that makes people feel better about the process. They weren't forgotten; they were being taken care of.

But honestly, lying is not ideal. Admitting our own shortcomings in a direct and self-deprecating way can actually bond you to a table better than dropping the standard lie, "The kitchen lost the ticket."

The Beauty of Stupid

The Art of War is the best book on service ever written. As Tzu says, "Appear weak when you are strong, and strong when you are weak."

This is not usually how I play it, but I have known plenty of successful servers who do it dumb. Playing the ditz makes you appear vulnerable. With specific tables, it helps when they feel superior. There is even a principle known as the "Damsel in Distress" effect. It states that people are more likely to "like" someone that they have to help.

Even the act of revealing an embarrassing detail about yourself tends to make people trust you more. The thinking is, why would you allow yourself to be vulnerable? You must be trustworthy.

The Seafood Tower

I recently found a piece on consumer behavior called "10 Ways to Convert More Customers Using Psychology" by Gregory Ciotti (@gregoryciotti). Reading it, I started to realize that much of it could be applied to selling a "seafood tower" or any "sampler platter."

A multi-tiered tower of raw bar may seem like an extravagant item, but they can really build out a check. So how can you sell it more often?

Reframe the Value: "It may be $175, but for a party of four that's less per person than if you each got your own thing. This way all of you get the option of more variety."

Bundling: People tend to buy more if they feel like they are "getting everything." "Getting the Tower allows you to try everything off the raw bar as opposed to just one or two items."

The Small Stuff: This may not work with the tower. But, thinking about how you talk about it in your script is essential. Even being able to say, "It's a great deal of food for the price" can push you into a sale. To quote Greggory Ciotti: "One of the goofiest conversion bumps ever is a study done by Carnegie Mellon University that reveals the impact of a single word on conversion rates. Researchers changed the description of an overnight shipping charge on a free DVD trial offer from "a $5 fee" to "a small $5 fee" and increased the response rate among tightwads by 20 percent."

The Fantasy Item

One benefit of getting to know the kitchen is discovering what they can do. I'm talking about all the snacks and off menu combos that the cooks cook for themselves. Knowing these off-menu mash-ups are good for many reasons. Sometimes you get a regular who wants to try something new. Sometimes you have a guest who wants something "exclusive." Having an unusual (but good) off-menu combo will make them feel special and excited.

Sometimes it's as simple as a customer who doesn't like what you have to offer. Knowing that your steak house can make a "veggie" platter using pickles, a beet salad, and some cheese can make all the difference.

This is now your cookie.

Make a cookie that you'd want to eat.

EXERCISES:

- **Make a list.** Make a list of all the standard requests, one-liners, and typical customer requests. Freewrite 100 answers, they don't have to be good. Consult on them with your coworkers. Compare and contrast.

- **Make New Friends.** Spend an afternoon approaching strangers asking for directions. Pay attention to things like eye contact, and voice levels, and shoes.

- **Read.** *Never Split the Difference* by Chris Vos, *Start with Why* by Simon Sinak, and *The Art of War* by Sun Tzu. For extra credit, check out Wikihow.com/Cold-Read

- **Internet.** The complete spoken works of Danny Meyer are available on YouTube. I'd also highly recommend the works of marketing guru Susan A. Friedmann (@nichepreneur). Start with her article "The 10 Commandments of Great Customer Service" from May 12, 2018, in *The Balance Small Business* blog.

❊ ❊ ❊

Cookies Recipe

> 1/2 cup butter (1 stick or 4 ounces / 113 grams)
> 1/3 cup + 1 tablespoon granulated sugar (5.73 ounces / 162 grams)
> 1/3 cup brown sugar, light or dark, packed (2.5 ounces / 71 grams)
> 1 large egg
> 1 teaspoon vanilla
> 1/2 teaspoon salt

1/4 teaspoon baking soda
1/2 teaspoon baking powder
1 1/2 cups All-Purpose Flour (6.375 ounces / 180 grams)
2 cups chocolate chips (any variety), nuts, raisins, and/or other dried fruit.

Start by creaming together cool (just below room temperature) butter and the sugar. Go until mixture is light and fluffy. Mix the wet ingredients. Add this mixture slowly to your creamed butter and sugar so that it incorporates fully. Sift or whisk together the dry ingredients. Add it in batches until thoroughly combined. Fold chips and/or assorted fruit and nuts into your batter.

Preheat the oven to 375°F. Line a couple of sheet pans with parchment paper. Then scoop the batter out by the tablespoonful, spacing them about 2" apart. Bake the cookies for about 12 minutes. Since oven can vary, go until they are golden brown with a touch of darkness around the edges.

THE FUCKING WORST

"Study Finds That All The Worst People Will Outlive You"

- THE ONION, HEADLINE 8.15.18

We've talked about going into a shift prepared for all the things that are supposed to happen. But, no matter how well you prepare for the usual stuff it's the unusual things that will make or break your shift.

In the course of my career, I have had customers grab me, insult me, yell in my face, and be drunk at me in 100 different ways. I have guarded coworkers against sexual assault and robbery. I've dodged wanted felons. I have vomited in the women's room sink and on the men's room door. I've accidentally smashed dishes, bottles, glasses, and once I dropped an entire tray of dirty dishes on a bodybuilder.

I have been at fault, and I have been faulted upon.

Some of what follows is small stuff. Some of it is big and serious. You may encounter none of it. But depending on where you work, you may see it every night.

Let's start small...

Apologizing

This is a fundamental requirement of life. But you'll need to use it regularly with both customers and staff. Channel your inner Canadian. It's going to suck sometimes, and there are going to be points where you know in your heart that you are correct. You need to be able to forgive and forget. That second part is going to particularly important when you know that you were in the right.

For me, I learned this first at the Cheesecake Factory, where my trainer laid out a simple technique early on. Her advice was to start every "no" with an "I'm so sorry..." It seems so dumb and simple, but it acknowledges that someone feels inconvenienced. Are they right? Most likely not, but using that phrase lets them feel like maybe they were.

Just don't forget that most people who go to eat in a restaurant have no idea how a restaurant works. Their crazy requests come from ignorance.

Accept that and move on.

The best guide I've seen to apologizing comes from YouTuber Emily Anderson (she's on Facebook too). Check her out for lots more perspective on the restaurant business, and don't forget to "RATE! COMMENT! SUBSCRIBE!" her.

Forgetting Things

Write stuff down. Even if you don't read it, it's insurance. If you do forget something and didn't have the opportunity to write it down, go back to a table and say you forgot. It's a lot better to look like a fool and get the order correct. Play it off as a matter of messy handwriting, or that you just needed to double check. If you don't fix the problem early, it will only cascade down the chain.

"Double checking" and looking like a fool for one second can be humbling, but most people appreciate it. Remember "The Beuty of Stupid"? This is that moment of vulnerability that will bring the table to your side. Besides, it's easier than ordering something on the fly later.

Sometimes you forgot an action, putting in an order or some such. There's a handy mental trick I've learned for when you can't remember if you did something. Concoct a weird phrase at the moment, and link it to your action.

An example: I'm working in a restaurant where I'm responsible for pouring wine at my table. As I plug in the order, I'll say something like "Cabernet Cabinet" to myself. That way, as I'm running around, scrolling through my todo list, and I'll hit table 44. The phrase will pop into my head as either a reminder or a confirmation.

"Did I put in the risotto for table 26?"

"Outrageous peaflap."

Yes! I did it!

Families (AKA Children)

I am not a parent, but I am an uncle. My goal is to train all my nieces and nephews to be a restaurant super-army. They'll give great hospitality, leave great tips, and eat all their vegetables and pâté. Of course, this means an army of toddlers is already training in the field.

If you have kids, you can skip this part. For the rest, I'll make it quick and easy.

Parents are going to go out to eat, and they are going to bring their kids. Be prepared to treat adults like adults. Then, give the kids enough attention to make them feel like they don't need to act out. The parents (especially new ones) will want to hang on to every moment of adulthood they can. You'll be their hero by talking to them like big boys and girls.

This is where your empathy skills come in. New parents, in particular, are very aware of the fact that everyone is looking at them and judging. They don't want to be on display any more than necessary. A table off to the side and in the back is often much appreciated. They should not feel ashamed, but they should feel comfortable to do what needs to get done.

Kids get bored. Having something ready to distract them will help. Crayons and paper will work. If you're feeling froggy, buy a gross of cheap birthday-goody-bag toys. It'll cost, like, $12, and it's worth the investment. You'll get a bit of that "principle of reciprocity" effect when it comes time for the check and tip.

Do you work in a place with no kid's menu? Take a moment to see if there aren't dishes on the menu that can be modified. Keep in mind that young children's taste buds are more receptive to sweet. Studies also show they're highly responsive to visual stimuli when eating. Buttered noodles on a funny plate or extra ketchup with a burger might be your secret weapon. But, just like with adults, every kid is different. Some toddlers eat oysters on the half-shell. I mean, a booger's a booger, right?

Have the check ready, and pay attention to their status. It's not about getting them to leave; it's about letting them feel like they have the freedom to bolt if things start leaking. Kids leak all the time. A lot of parents want the freedom to leave as much as they want their freedom to be out.

Kids are a part of the consumer equation. Remember Joe Camel? He was a cartoon used to inspire children to smoke. Just like with Joe, our goal is to get them while they're young. There are restaurants I went to as a child that I still frequent today. Parents will also remember a positive experience. When they finally get a babysitter, they'll come back sans child and drink *all* of the wine.

Be prepared to sweep under the table when they leave. Don't judge. Just know where the broom is.

Campers

In Russia they have Ziferblat. It's labeled as an "anti-cafe." "Ziferblat is a pay per minute social space, used as an alternative to a coffee house, coworking space or a lounge." The basic idea is that you're paying for a comfortable space to exist in. Paying to "exist" in the US hasn't happened yet, and restaurants here don't carry an idling charge — yet. But maybe they should?

Campers are the people who refuse the economic reality which requires people to chew and screw. Fact is, volume is one of the biggest determiners of a restaurant's success or failure. More people in less time is one reason why the restaurant business loves "fast casual." But rushing people out is usually considered antithetical to hospitality. So how do you handle this?

I once had a manager who swore that throwing salt on the ground by the table would get people to go. I can't say that's brought me much success.

I knew one server who'd command that any table with a check presenter on the table was not to get any more water. This seems a bit severe. Clearing tables and doing a wipe down works to an extent, but if they're nursing drinks that only does so much. It may seem awkward at first, but removing the signed credit slip or change with a loud and enthusiastic, "THANK YOU!" works too.

Cut time where you can. Especially in the beginning because that's when you have the most influence and flexibility. It is possible to greet tables, get drinks and orders in quickly, without being rude.

Some restaurants won't seat incomplete parties. But, if they do, something that moves stuff along is greeting early arrivals. Ask if they want a drink while they're waiting for the rest of their party[3]. If someone already has a drink down when the rest of the party arrives, it encourages them all to order drinks. It signals that "The meal has started. Let's get on with it."

It also helps to know your shit. The fewer trips you have to make to ask questions or check on things, the faster you can get orders in, and food down.

At certain places, people are told in advance that their time at a table is limited. I like having a table that understands this reality because nine times out of 10 they want to help with the process.

If the house is pressed for seating, sometimes just suggesting a dessert in a to-go bag is the perfect touch. Will, any of these tricks work? Maybe not. But that's when your ability to apologize comes in handy.

"I'm so sorry. I need you all to GTFO."

Getting Overwhelmed

Especially if you're new to the field, anxiety can creep in. It happens all the time. Embracing the feeling can help you get past it. Don't use it as a crutch, but if you're feeling anxious, admit your anxiety to a coworker. Saying it aloud can sometimes ease the stress. If you're saying it aloud to people all the time, you should consider re-strategizing how you work. Or... find a different career path.

Everyone who works in restaurants gets overwhelmed. Most of us have personal ways to deal with it, but it's important to know when to ask for help. Ask politely, and return the favor when you can. A good manager should be able to assist you in a pinch, or at the very least be able to find someone who can.

Speaking of management, there is a management trick used to get people to help. If you need something done, politely say, "Start with this task," as opposed to "Do this task." It's a small psychological trigger where it presumes the "yes." If you presume people will help you, it makes them more likely to do it.

If you want to get sneaky, talk to someone while handing them something. The action distracts them, and at that moment you split their attention between a physical act and a mental task. This will make them more pliable, and now you're more apt to get an affirmative answer.

Passive Aggression

There's a tremendous amount of passive aggression in restaurants. Not reading your back issues of *Psychology Today*? Passive aggression is described as a "covert way to express feelings of anger." In restaurants, it's the result of anger or frustration a person feels that they can't express in public.

When it comes to co-workers, be aware of it. Treat it in the same way as the "Shitty People" section below. Accept it. Treat the offender with kindness, (to a point), and move on.

Much more common is a customer who is easily embarrassed and who doesn't know how to handle those feelings. We tend to forget this because it's such an integral part of our jobs, but placing an order is an act of public speaking. This is a lot of people's greatest fear. With an order, people are expected to make a public judgment call to a stranger. It seems like a small act, but some people find it nerve-wracking.

Some feel slighted if a waiter corrects their pronunciation of a dish's name. Or, they may feel uncomfortable about declaring that they have a food allergy. If a person makes a special request, and they feel you've shut them down without listening, they'll tend to fight back with passive-aggressive behavior. This shows up in eye-rolls, rude requests, or the questioning of your ability. They'll say things like, "Are you sure this is a medium burger?"

Remember these people are strangers, and you have no idea what they're dealing with. Judging their actions (no matter how ludicrous they seem) won't do you much good.

One typical response from the passive-aggressively inclined is that they let problems escalate. For example, if the dish didn't come out the way they wanted, these people sit and stew as opposed to complaining. These are the people who eat the wrong food when it's placed in front of them. These are the people who hate something, won't say anything until they get home, and then they let-it-rip on Yelp. Yelp is the ultimate weapon of the passive-aggressive. It allows people to exact public revenge from a private position.

If these people feel particularly wronged, they might steal serviceware or decorations. I've seen it happen. Or they might smear their feces on the wall of a Howard Johnson's bathroom stall.

I've seen it happen.

To combat this behavior, you need to eliminate the gratification from exacting revenge. Your best bet is to show composure. Use things like humor, be humble, and elevate the guest. Show them that you take their requests, no matter how odd they may seem, seriously.

Then, laugh things off. Tell a joke. If they complain to you about something, stay present. Listen to them, and remember that you don't have to agree or disagree immediately. Let them know that you'll keep what they've said in mind. Then get on with what you need to get on with. Resist the temptation to respond with blunt aggression. Being politely assertive and confident are your best weapons.

It's important to note that I have no psychological training. But I did read the Signe Whitson L.S.W article, "Understanding Passive Aggressive Behavior," in *Psychology Today*.

Everyone walks in carrying some baggage. You won't be able to fix every problem. Maintaining perspective will help you recover when someone acts out.

Brunch and Other High Demand Shifts

There are certain shifts that people need to be aware of. Mother's day. Valentine's Day. New Years (Eve and Day). Sunday Brunch. All these shifts have something in common. They're not only expected to be meals, but they're also expected to be "experiences."

Each of these occasions is expected to be shared with the most important people in someone's life. Each has its own set of issues to navigate. There are wave seatings, cocktail specials, prix fixe menus, and many "specials." I can't cover every possibility, but being aware of what your restaurant is doing, well in advance, is crucial.

The most frequent of these high demand shifts is brunch. It was 1895 when Guy Beringer, an English writer, suggested a new meal to take the edge off of Saturday night. A sprawling social affair, he coined the term "Brunch." This meal can be about family, but it's usually the weekend's excuse to get together with friends.

It's Saturday Night for the older, coupled, crowd.

Shawn Micallef (@shawnmicallef), author of, *The Trouble With Brunch: Work, Class, and the Pursuit of Leisure* describes the meal this way:

> *"Empathy, I observed, does not exist at brunch. Diners linger over cooling, almost empty cups of Lapsang souchong even as people waiting for a table stand in conspicuous view. There is no inclination to clear out and let others enjoy their time here. Brunchers treat servers uncharitably and servers, in turn, view them with contempt."*

The key to all these shifts is managing expectations. Your biggest problem is guests who want more than what a restaurant can accommodate. They want a grand and important meal. You, on the other hand, want to quit working at The Cheesecake Factory[4].

My best advice? Get a good night's rest. Eat a light but healthy breakfast. Listen to you "pump-up playlist." Get to work early. Make sure all of the coffee machines are working. Be the happiest fucking person you can be before the shift begins.

Be fucking bulletproof.

Be ready for oceans of passive-aggressive behavior. Be prepared for children. Be prepared for kitchen failures. Be ready to apologize, and make sure you're prepared to tell people "no" in the nicest way possible.

Shitty People

There will always be shitty customers (clients, assholes). There are just so many of them. But, you might also find yourself dealing with some crappy coworkers. This happens even in an otherwise stellar work environment. Some people are dealing with things and can't keep them out of a job.

Some people are just shitty. Since you can't control any of them, learn how to deal with it on your end.

If you're in the middle of an incident, the most effective hit back is to say something nice about a person. You must be sincere. It's disarming. It fights fire with water. It also pulls a psychological pin in your brain, making you more apt to think better of them. I'm not saying you'll start loving them, but you'll be in a better, healthier, headspace.

Especially with coworkers, you can take advantage of the "Ben Franklin Effect." That's when you borrow something from a person who doesn't like you (think wine key or pen). This triggers cognitive dissonance in people. They feel like they wouldn't do you a favor unless they liked you. Again, not a magic bullet, but it's a chip away at the wall.

Don't have time for the casual approach? Look at the middle of someone's head, just above the bridge of their nose. Or stare at their shoes. Both of these approaches, especially while in a conversation, will make the other person self-conscious. The more they think about themselves, the less they'll think about you.

If someone is actively hostile, try standing next to that person. Stand side to side, not face to face. This makes people feel uncomfortable and can put a damper on aggression. This works particularly well if an antagonist is sitting at a table.

If none of this makes the problem subside, and you can't have a peaceful discussion, it's time to talk to a manager. Good managers should be empathetic enough to listen without judgment. Then they'll offer solutions.

If someone is abusing you, another customer or a coworker, skip right to management. You don't have time for that shit, nor does the restaurant.

Something to always keep in your back pocket is the knowledge that it's difficult to change someone's mind. If someone has targeted you as "the bad guy," it makes the most sense to let it go. If you have to, ask if the table can be transferred. Your best point of attack is to make sure all the other tables in your section are having the best time possible.

Living well is the best revenge.

Lastly, there's the "name game." There was a point where it was expected that a server give their name at the start of a meal. Many places have shyed away from this artifice, and frankly, I prefer its absence. Occasionaly a table will ask me for my name.

In a hostage situation, giving your name to your captor is supposed to humanize you. It's supposed to make it harder for them to abuse you. So maybe giving your name is a good thing?

The problem is that a lot of customers misuse this. They take your name and use it as a bludgeon. Suddenly people start yelling across a crowded restaurant, "HEY, MIKE!"

Like a quality stripper, I often prefer to use a fake name. I used to work with a "Batman." He had the right idea. No reasonable adult yells, "HEY, BATMAN!" across a crowded restaurant.

Of course, the unreasonable assholes will yell it all fucking night long.

Allergies

Any smart restaurant has a specific and detailed allergy protocol. Learn the ins and outs of how your restaurant handles this stuff.

There are absolutely people with fake allergies who claim that they can't have gluten. Then, they'll throw back a rack of beer. People will say they are deathly allergic to mayonnaise or cilantro when they simply don't like it. As annoying as it is dealing with these fakers, you have to field all allergy requests seriously.

Here's a story from a friend of mine.

At the front end of his career, he got a job tending bar in a seafood restaurant. Still new to the job, one of his coworkers introduced him to one of the restaurant's longtime regulars as he sat down at the bar. My friend and the regular exchanged greetings. A drink was ordered, along with a dish. Time passed, and the food arrived.

Distractedly the regular started to eat. Suddenly he turned to my friend and asked if there was shellfish in the dish.

There was.

The regular grabbed a napkin and started to write. He then placed a phone call. Lastly, he calmly explained to my friend that he had a severe shellfish allergy. A lawyer, he had written what amounted to a "release form" on the cocktail napkin. He did it to release my friend and the restaurant of all liability. The call he placed was for an ambulance. He made it to the hospital just in time to slip into a week-long coma.

Thankfully, he survived.

This scared the shit out of my friend. Rightfully so.

Now, some of you are asking, *"Why the fuck didn't the guy say something if he was in a fucking seafood restaurant?"*

The answer? As a regular customer, he had assumed that he was safe. In the past, he'd been well taken care of. They had a system in place where he had always felt safe ordering, so safe, he didn't give it a second thought. My friend had assumed that when his coworker mentioned to him that this was a regular, he would have specified if he had an allergy. As such, my friend didn't think to ask.

It was a shitty situation where there wasn't one person to blame. It was a breakdown in communication.

Allergies are relevant because you don't know when and where they will strike. Customers often assume that they can surmise what's in a dish by looking at the menu, and this isn't always the case. It's your job to be as aware as possible and always ask questions of the customers and of the kitchen.

On top of allergies, you also have dietary restrictions. I've worked in places where the vegetable dishes have fish sauce. Some fish sauces contain shellfish; others don't. You should be able to tell if vegetarians, vegans, pescatarians, and finfish or shellfish allergy folks can order the broccoli.

I once had a hallal customer order a venison dish that came covered in lardo. When asked during the ordering process if he had any, "allergies or dietary restrictions," he replied, "No." When the dish arrived the server mentioned it had lardo. He said he didn't know what lardo was. Once explained that it was pork fat, he became irate. He had assumed that a dish labeled "venison" would be safe.

Ever since then, I go out of my way to mention that, "not every ingredient is listed on the menu." This should seem obvious, but again, some customers get self-conscious when ordering. This phrase has weeded out a handful of last minute, dangerous, food allergies over the years.

I once got chewed out by a customer because they had a fish allergy. I asked if they were okay with "cross-contamination," which is the BOH term for various foods being prepared with the same equipment. Think of a flat-top used to cook fish and then beef. Or, a deep fryer used to fry peanuts and then hours later used to make french fries.

The word "contamination" made her bristle. She yelled at me, "Well if it's not clean. Maybe I shouldn't eat here!" I talked her down, but ever since I've used the more friendly sounding, "How are you for food prepared on 'shared-surfaces?'"

Talk to your tables and be honest without being condescending. There is gluten in soy sauce. They may not like the taste of cilantro, but since it's the same thing as coriander, at some places a "cilantro allergy" will eliminate half the menu. As such, I've had more than a few "Visible Cilantro Allergies." Practice your straight face, and be willing to spend the time talking to people.

There's only so much you can do, but do what you can. There are things like ServSafe, WebMD, and even Wikipedia has a decent list of food allergies.

Drunks

Much like children, drunks require extra attention. The problem is that drunk adults are dangerous. Our first job as a people selling alcohol is to prevent customers from getting too drunk in the first place.

But sometimes they come in drunk. Or friends send them drinks, or it otherwise escalates unexpectedly. In that case, it's a triage situation. You must assess and determine the best course of action.

How is the person? Are they Grumpy? Happy? Sleepy? Angry? Dopey? Vomity?

The intoxicated person needs to be taken care of. In some ways, they're in the perfect place. They need water. Keep them hydrated. Caffeine is good too if they are nodding off, but remember coffee doesn't sober you up, it only makes you more awake. Food is good. I've sent bread, crackers, and chips to drunks (for free). Food slows down the absorption of alcohol. Though, if they are already blitzed, it may be a bit late for this.

Retching is a bad sign. If I even think I see a dry heave building, it's time to get that person to a bathroom. I have a responsibility to everyone paying for dinner in that restaurant. If one customer loses it... I don't want to recreate the blueberry pie scene from *Stand By Me*.

The only acceptable "splash zone" is around the porcelain throne.

Remember: Dealing with a drunk is a team sport. Make sure your coworkers have an eye on them too. This means the bartenders, bussers, managers — everyone. Everyone needs to be aware of what is happening. If a customer has been cut-off, you don't want the bar selling them a "quick shot." If another waiter hears a stomach burble, they might be able to help get them to the facilities faster. Most Important — if they're with a group, you want the group on your side. These people are your greatest asset. Friends will have an easier time convincing drunks to slow down or alter behavior.

When cutting them off, have a plan in place. Let the manager know that they need to be cut-off. Management will be your enforcer. When it comes time, be empathetic and kind. You are looking out for them. Lean on the fact that their behavior is risking your livelihood. If the restaurant loses its liquor license, you could be out of a job. Liquor Board fines are no joke.

Full disclosure: I have been the drunk asshole. 96.2% of the time I wish I'd been cut-off before I got to that point.

Is there yelling? Screaming? Stealing drinks from friends? Tell them to go. Drunks are not known for their reasoning ability so don't reason with them. Be calm and direct. Tell them the facts. They must leave. IF THERE IS VIOLENCE (OR A THREAT) OF ANY KIND, CALL THE COPS.

Decompress with your coworkers after your shift with a zesty lemonade.

Addendum: Make sure the intoxicated person is safe. Be aware of things like GHB and Rohypnol (date rape drugs) which can speed up the effects of alcohol. If someone goes from sober to drunk on one drink, question what's happening. Be aware.

There are all sorts of courses that will expand your knowledge of how to handle these issues. When it comes to alcohol safety courses, there's a state by state chart at servingalcohol.com.

Robberies and Other Emergencies

You can take courses on CPR and in other emergency medicine, and of course, there's a wide variety of martial arts training available. My friend once worked with a martial arts expert who was also a server. One night this martial artist disarmed a drunk and unruly patron with a handgun. As he did so, the gun fired into the parking lot asphalt. It was big and dramatic, and it no doubt ruined an otherwise pastoral night at The Olive Garden.

I've also had a couple of friends who worked at a chain pizza restaurant that was regularly robbed at gunpoint. No injuries reported, but everyone lost their cash. Now that restaurants don't operate with as much money these days, some of these events are less frequent.

All that said, at the end of the day, our job is dinner. Stay low. Keep your head. Call 911.

Sexual Harassment

Never tolerate it. It's just a job.

In the US you can register a complaint with the Equal Employment Opportunity Commission (usually within 180-300 days). Then there's RAINN which operates a National Sexual Assault Telephone Hotline at 800-656-HOPE (4673).

Racism

Nope.

There are big obvious things and small insidious things, but restaurants seem to separate along a pretty stark divide when it comes to race and position.

Take the time to read this paper put out by Restaurant Opportunities Centers United: *Ending Jim Crow in America's Restaurants: Racial and Gender Occupational Segregation in the Restaurant Industry.*

Give it a Google. It's available free. Ignorance is not bliss.

A Generally Terrible Workplace

It happens. Most restaurants are fine. Some are a bad fit, and some are freakishly terrible. If you're lucky you find the one. You settle down and franchise. For the rest, you call the cops and walk away with a good story.

Never be afraid to walk away if you feel your safety is being threatened.

EXERCISES:

- **Read the SPIKES Protocol.** In what may seem to be the most unusual advice I give, I'd ask that you read the SPIKES Protocol. Developed by Doctor Rob Buckman, it's a six-step process designed for delivering bad news. Specifically, it's designed to deal with things like diabetes and cancer. But it also has some remarkable service applications. SPIKES helps the doctor gather information from the patient, then give that information back. It then provides support for the patient, and it gets them to then collaborate in developing a strategy for the future. Reading this may seem like overkill, but if you've dealt with a "Hangry Becky," you know that sometimes avocado toast is like cancer. You should also learn more about Dr. Buckman and the development of SPIKES. Listen to episode 306: "Breaking Bad News" of the podcast, *99% Invisible*. Then, fall down 99%'s perfectly constructed rabbit-hole (garnished with a plaque) and subscribe.

- **Take a ServSafe course.** Some restaurants require it, but mostly it's just some useful and practical things to know.

- **Learn CPR or other emergency medicine.** Again, isn't this just a fun excuse to learn more about how to be a cooler and more useful human being?

- **Take a martial arts course.** I want to stress: I am not advocating that anyone disarm a robber. No one should insert themselves into a fight. But, discipline, control, and the ability to defend yourself when walking home at 3 AM after your bar shift? Priceless.

FUCKING
MANAGEMENT

"Recently, I really wanted to learn the operations on the other side of the bar, in the dining room. So they made me Restaurant Supervisor. I still run the bar, so I do all the ordering, inventory, and training, I just don't bartend anymore. I now run the restaurant. I'm three months in and I fucking hate it. I always thought I wanted to be a Restaurant Manager and I now realize that I don't. I inherited 10 times the responsibility and half the pay. I have loved my job for a long time because of my passion for bartending, and now I dread coming to work every single day. I was so good at my job. I was stupid to leave it but I thought I had learned all I could. Everyone used to think of me as happy and fun, now everyone thinks I'm nasty and mean. I'm miserable doing this. I cry twice a week due to stress."

- U/TINIESTTURTLES
IN THE R/BARTENDERSSECTION OF REDDIT

Restaurant management is an odd job. The boundaries of expertise are not well defined, but it helps to be a jack of all trades. It means calmly absorbing endless requests and demands from staff and customers. A restaurant manager's main job is to reinforce each weak point in the system right before it explodes.

As a server, a manager can be the difference between a good job and a nightmare clown swamp. How management treats staff is what dictates the tone of the restaurant.

In most high-end-independent restaurants new managers get little training. They also make less money than the waitstaff, all while working longer hours with fewer prospects for internal advancement. In return, they gain respect (outside of their place of employment). On the plus side, most high-end-independent restaurants attract more seasoned talent. This makes the manager's job easier when it comes to directly managing the staff.

Becoming a manager at Fridays or Chili's is roundly mocked. But it also pays better, offers more training and support, and there's lots of opportunity for growth. The downside is a less invested staff which can make every shift a cat-herding hellscape.

Sometimes the corporate manager will enter a smaller restaurant feeling that their training makes them more qualified. Different restaurants require different skill sets. Corporate restaurants usually need less expertise in the kind of nitty-gritty problems smaller operations face; corporate joints need someone who can handle bureaucracy.

In short, being a restaurant manager sucks. The good ones recognize this fact, are willing to learn and adapt. They too use empathy to get things done, but for them, it's all about empathy for the staff[5].

To give you a "compact" and concrete overview of restaurant management I've adapted the 1981 song "88 Lines About 44 Women" from the band The Nails. It's a brief examination of some (not all) of the managers I have known. (Deepest apologies to The Nails.)

"88 lines about 44 Managers"

Devin was my first boss,
He stole cash and then got fired.

This is a problem that I've encountered with more than a few managers over the years: sticky fingers. Some of them seemed great, but this can be a punishing job. It tends to engender bitterness. What's worse is that this was a trickle-down situation. Most of his staff was stealing too: everything from liquor to food, to cash and prizes.

Carlo was a different type,
former cop, who then got hired.

This is going to get me a lot of flack, but I don't like working for ex-cops. I'll work for ex-military any day of the week, but cops are a different breed. Most seem to carry with them an element of suspicion that runs counter to empathy and gets in the way of a service industry orientation.

Barry had the worst teeth.
Breath was bad but good with numbers.

Some managers have the job because they understand the business, even if they don't understand people. Barry was destined to work his way up the corporate restaurant ladder and is doing very well for himself.

Susan was a former waitress,
female boss, not unencumbered.

As much as I dislike working for ex-cops, I love working for former waitresses. They are usually the funniest, most capable people on the planet. They are often good at what they do because they've put up with the most shit. They've seen everything, and they are aikido masters when it comes to exploiting leverage.

Chip was a fresh new hire,
always gave his résumé.

"Noob" managers are easy to spot because they need to exert authority. This rears its head in many ways. Sometimes it's plain micromanagement. Often they'll mention all the other places they've worked or mention how hard they worked to get where they are.

Donnie was a cocaine freak,
He ate hot dogs locked away.

Again, a lot of longtime managers get bitter. If they aren't embezzling, sometimes they steal food and binge eat. Some do massive amounts of drugs. Almost always they take advantage of rooms with locking doors. A manager who plays with a ring of keys is someone to be wary of.

Chris had unique skills,
disappeared when he drank.

The great conflict for restaurant managers everywhere is that they often want to be friends with their staff. To some extent, they should be. A good manager always knows where their employee's heads are at. But, like a therapist, there should be professional distance. The problem comes when they go out drinking with them. Managers should be close, but not too close. The true masters of the art, like "Chris", show up for a beer, occasionally pay for a round of shots, but they are never there for last call.

Caesar was the worst ever.
Bought a boat. I hope it sank.

Embezzlement. It happens a lot. Again, keep an eye out for old white guys with odd food habits and who spend all their time in the office. This one, in particular, was a particularly pungent example of management dictating a restaurant adversely. He used to yell at customers, and I was always apologizing for him. He was the GM of the worst restaurant I ever worked at.

Jacob was a real smart guy,
Changed it up to selling vino.

Good managers can usually get a much better job as a liquor rep, with higher pay, shorter hours, and more perks.

Joan had lots of confidence,
but no skills of that which we know.

Unfortunately, restaurant management has many examples of "The Peter Principle." This rule states that "In a hierarchy, every employee tends to rise to his level of incompetence." Being a great waiter is no sign of how good a manager one will be. In the case of Joan, she was only promoted because she spoke Italian (it was an Italian restaurant). She was not only fired, but after she left it was revealed that she'd been fired from nearly every other restaurant job she'd ever had.

Damon was a satanist.
His band? First priority.

For whatever reason, I've found that a lot of managers hired from within the restaurant have a band on the side. They got into the business because of the hours, and when the band didn't take off, they became managers to feed the kids. They're good because the job is just a job to them. At all times they would rather be playing in their band.

Dani lied to get her job,
and told my ex to fuck with me.

Many managers get their job by saying they managed at another restaurant when they haven't. It rarely matters. This is a business where a lot of restaurant managers will vouch for a friend's fictional resume. Of course, since many restaurant managers are just servers with titles and keys, they will try too hard to be friends with the staff. Again, always beware of the keys.

Goodwin was a happy drunk.
He never stopped the entertaining.

Drinking is a curse that runs rampant in the restaurant industry. A lot of managers become highly skilled at hiding their problem. Sometimes they conceal it by bringing everyone else along with them in a never-ending nightmare party.

Donald liked to fuck at work,
in the liquor room, his veins were straining.
Roary was his side piece,
she conceived amidst the bottles.
Bill had code to stay away.
He didn't want to see their wattles.

Managers are people too, and they have wants and needs. I can't tell you the number of marriages ruined by long hours and proximity to other lonely people. Sometimes it's other managers. Sometimes it's staff. Sometimes it's customers. Not every manager who does this is a creep. But there is a lot of creepiness in the business. Add to that; there's the fact that when the staff fornicates at the restaurant someone probably knows. If one person knows, everyone knows.

Harry was the last adult,
rolled his eyes at child like mobs.

It's hard to be a restaurant manager and also behave like an adult. The hours are absurd, the pay is nonsense, and you are surrounded by a never-ending flow of drunks and teenagers. Perspective is hard when you're cleaning up after a perpetual party with kids who don't want to pay attention.

Willie was a former lawyer.
Get him drunk? He'd give out jobs!

Along with drunks and children, restaurant management also tends to suck in those who have burned out of another career path. Not a good or bad thing, but it demonstrates that restaurants are always and forever the fallback position.

Darryl kept real damn quiet,
I still think he's there, you know?

Sometimes the most effective management style is "uninvolved." In that state, you don't usually move up, but you can also stay detached enough to raise a family and live a "normal" life. They may not be dynamic, but as an employee, they can be very easy to work for. They'll tell you precisely what they want from you, and they are very low drama. They often work opening shifts.

Roberto came and went so fast,
t'was immigration made him go.

No one will ever be able to convince me that undocumented immigrants aren't worth fighting for. Many of them would be great managers if only they were allowed to be. I often see them relegated to "honorary" management positions due to "paperwork issues." In these positions, they make less than their embezzling, native-born, counterparts.

Jackie was a Boston transplant,
Came for glory. Stayed for cash.

The managers in bands and the ones who come from other professions, usually wind up in corporate restaurants. They get shuttled around and have no great love of restaurants. The chains know this, and they break out the "golden handcuffs" because these people are only in it for the paycheck.

Papi wore dark, thick, eyeliner,
was always jumpy at the pass.

The position of "restaurant manager" isn't set in stone. As such you have people in the post who have no idea how to do the jobs they wind up doing. A key example of this is how many restaurants wind up with managers expediting food. A food expeditor is the conductor of the kitchen. They dictate how an order comes together. The problem comes when you have an incredible host who gets promoted to management, and then suddenly they have to lead a kitchen. Maybe they can do it, perhaps they can't, but it seems you always find out at the worst time.

Lindon born with just two limbs,
kept the kitchen running smoothly.

The best Kitchen Manager I ever worked with in a corporate chain was born with one arm and one leg. He could jump on the line like a mofo, and he was funny, smart, and capable. No insight here, just a great guy.

Roger was much too goofy,
stayed obsessed with our white shoes.
Uh huh, "cheeser" forever.

Some managers are incapable of authority. They are regularly caught off guard. Their bosses often undermine them, and as a result, they take it out on the staff by complaining about small things. These are things that probably don't matter, but he has just enough authority to make it stick. You will often find them lurking at major chain restaurants.

Paul thought that he was the greatest,
drove us to insanity.

More of the above. He was an ex-cop who used what authority he had to make oversized dictums designed to assert his power.

Jordan, GM, rarely there,
for some reason he liked me.

A good restaurant GM is there when they need to be, and a ghost when they are not. If they are always there, it shows a lack of trust. If they are never there, it shows a lack of interest. Striking a balance is hard. The other problem is that it's nearly impossible to be there the "right" amount of time for everyone. The outstanding managers don't care what you think, but they make you believe that they do.

Kevin was a perfect boss,
he could coax me off a bridge.

I can count on one hand the managers where I would do exactly what they asked of me without thought or question. That comes from trust, and you get trust by not only giving it but being able to call out nonsense. Smelling bullshit and gauging a proportional response is a superpower belonging to great restaurant management.

Kelly was a rich punk rocker,
kept no booze within her fridge.

Managers who stare at the edge of drug and alcohol oblivion and then come back dry, are a fascinating breed. Being able to stay in the business after that is like being a celiac baker or a diabetic candy maker (I've worked with all of these btw). Every day you're confronted with a certain amount of danger. It can make you sober and severe, but sometimes it makes you disciplined and smart.

Sarah was a polymath,
She could do everything.

BOH managers feel very different from FOH managers. In the BOH it is not uncommon for the managers to hop in and help dig people out. FOH managers get their authority through delegation. They'll throw you a preserver, but they don't jump in the water. Add to that; some FOH managers are downright terrible servers. In the kitchen setting, a manager can nearly always do the job better than those under them.

Janet was smarter still,
Undid messes in the bin.

I once messed up a large batch of pita bread dough, and Janet was able to figure out where I went wrong, and fixed it, just by weighing my mess. She managed to undo my boo-boo without making me feel like a dumb-dumb. She was a perfect example of BOH manager greatness.

Wendy wondered when she'd sleep,
she worked like a gal possessed.

I recently had a conversation with a friend of mine who's the GM of a major chain restaurant. She believes that managers who are there all the time are often burning themselves into martyrdom because they have issues at home. The job becomes an excuse. If you want to avoid your homelife, restaurant management is the place to be.

Brando's penchant for dick swinging,
left him angry and undressed.

This was an example of toxic masculinity, drug use, alcoholism, and mental illness. He was also a very talented cook. He made everyone around him feel stupid. It was terrible. I only wish he'd left the restaurant business sooner.

Rowena didn't like me much,
thought I was dumber than a fuck.

There is no bigger disappointment than when your boss has no faith in your abilities. It's even worse when they let you know it. The crazy truth is that you'll occasionally find managers who can't fire you. Instead, they'll do whatever they can to make you feel uncomfortable in the hopes that you'll quit. It happens more than you'd think.

Joey was her better half,
He was nice, but still a schmuck.

I've worked for some romantically linked business partners. Sometimes it works. Sometimes it doesn't. The problem is if it's not working, they are much less likely to get fired or quit.

Debbie, calm, cool, collected,
had the long term on her mind.

Another sign of a good manager is one who has perspective.

Manager turnover is about as bad as the rest of the business. The ability to be in the moment, appreciate the work, but understanding that it's all temporary, is a strength.

Nina, she was just a baby,
now she is the mother kind.

Some people fall into a management position and grow into the role. They listen, they learn, and then they get better. I have seen terrible managers become great at the job. A manager is there to back you up, but sometimes it also goes in reverse.

Bobbi was a bit dramatic,
lost her cool, but she was fun.

I have worked with a lot of managers in their first managing job. One of the hardest things I've seen noobs deal with over and over is how to keep the lid on. As servers, you can bitch to your coworkers, but that doesn't fly in a management position. Learning how to release frustration and anger is both a talent and a learned skill.

Mike the nice and quirky spastic,
pooka shells, the bearded one.

Sometimes your "manager in a band" doesn't get angry when frustrated. Sometimes they turn the anger inward and become scattered and easily confused. For these guys you look them dead in the eye, smile, mirror some deep breaths their way, and Sullivan nod them into a calm state of serenity.

Terri didn't give a shit.
Was just a nihilist.

Some managers don't care. Sometimes they seem like they're looking to get fired. Often though, being fired would devastate them. These are people who appear to feel both taken advantage of and bulletproof. They believe that no one else could do (or would want to do) their job. As such, they engage in risky behavior. This is often the step before alcoholism, drug abuse, and embezzlement.

Igor was blind yet smart,
Never saw just what he missed.

Like I said before, some managers get their job because they have a particular set of skills (cost management, promotions, service). Managers who've been in the business for a while sometimes succumb to the Peter Principle. Suddenly they have to master a skill set that they never had to before. Sometimes that big hurdle is merely the act of hiring other managers. Lousy management staff is a simple shortcoming that can destroy a restaurant.

Jezebel went forty days,
Drinking nothing but Islay.

Alcoholism is real. Managers can often find free drinks all over town. Add to that, their intimate knowledge of liquor costs can be a handy way to squeeze extra alcohol from the workplace.

Dino drove his restaurant,
into the Massachusetts Bay.

At this point in my career, it's a checklist. With Dino, it was the Peter Principle. Alcoholic. Poor hiring skills. There are ways to come back from this. The problem - can a manager ask for help? Whom do they ask?

Judy came from just up north,
Fell for her as if possessed!

I do not believe in love at first sight, but that's how I would describe my job interview with this one. We'd have been terrible romantic partners, but when it comes to restaurants, we seemed to be on the same wavelength.

Just for Victor, here's a kiss,
I chose you to end this list.

Sometimes you have coworker friends who become manage-ment. Sometimes you watch them explode, but if you're lucky, you get to watch them succeed. I've worked with this particular person across three restaurants, and I wouldn't be upset if there were a fourth.

EXERCISES:

- **Interview a Restaurant Manager.** Don't talk to your current boss, and they won't be able to have a full, free and open conversation with you. Instead, get to know a manager in another restaurant. Ask them for stories, advice and more. Make them your mentor. They can be the person you talk to when you are afraid of your boss.

- **Go out to eat.** Can you spot the manager? Are they on the floor? How are they handling themselves in the dining room? Watch how the staff interacts with them. Where are people's eyes, arms, and how are their feet positioned. Is the manager in control? Do they seem stressed?

FUCKING TIPS

"Treat what you don't have as nonexistent. Look at what you have, the things you value most, and think of how much you'd crave them if you didn't have them. But be careful. Don't feel such satisfaction that you start to overvalue them — that it would upset you to lose them."

— MARCUS AURELIUS, MEDITATIONS

This is the chapter that most people want when they pick up a book about "being a better waiter." If you want to make more money, and you work in the US, that means you looking for bigger tips.

There are suggestions throughout this book that will help you with tips in subtle ways. The harder question to ask is whether the tipping system is helping or hurting the business. I've passively researched tips for 20 years, but when I decided to write this book, I put in some hard research.

It didn't take long for me to consider throwing this entire book away.

In the business, talking about tips is a little like talking about religion or politics. Servers both defend and bemoan the process while everyone else feels like they aren't getting a fair cut. At the heart of the debate: What are a person's time and attention worth? What's their knowledge worth? How much of their income is tied to other people's work? Are those other people being appropriately compensated? How much of a server's paycheck is total luck, and has nothing to do with them at all?

Restaurant customers rarely know what their food and service are worth, and they do not know how to judge these things accurately. It's not that they couldn't understand it. It's that a lot of what makes good service "good" is stuff you aren't supposed to notice. Restaurants are also set up in such a way that ideally a customer will get a nearly identical experience regardless of who waits on them.

If we stopped to explain everything that was happening, it would take longer than the meal. So instead we default to a system of trust. But have restaurants respected that trust? Should the public be paying the servers? Should it be the employers?

Employers argue that tipping allows them to employ more people. They argue that this improves restaurant growth and the overall economy. But, if letting employees work for donations is the only way to make the business viable, is it a viable business?

After doing a lot more research into this than I thought I would. The answer I've arrived at is... "It's very complicated, and you should do your own research".

When people like Danny Meyer are trying to fight the problems inherent in the system, and finding it incredibly difficult, what are the chances that I will figure it out in a book with a curse word in the title?

As long as tipping is how things work, there are some things every tipped employee should know.

Where the Fuck Did Tipping Come From?

In 2013 *The Atlantic* reported that "TIP" is an acronym that arose in London in 1754, at a Fleet Street coffee shop. It was short for, "To Insure Promptitude." As of January 2018, *Snopes.com* claims the phrase "To insure promptness," and its alternatives ("To Insure Performance," "To Insure Prompt Service") is a load of hooey.

Snopes offers the following explanation:

"...the use of tip to describe the act of giving something to another (where that list of possible 'somethings' could include small sums of money, intelligence on horse races, or the latest silly joke) goes back to 1610. Tip slipped into the language as underworld slang, with the verb 'to tip' (meaning 'to give to or share with') being used by shady characters as part of the then-current argot of petty criminals."

In other words, it was shady slang, and it implied using cash to "tip" the odds in your favor.

Another story often passed around is that the term comes from "tipple," as the act was often linked to drinks. In many other languages, the word for tipping seems to come down to some variation of "drink money."

But all this is just about the origin of the word...

Where Does the Practice Originate?

For a full history of this practice read *Tipping* by Kerry Seawell. Beware, it tends towards the dry and academic. For a more activist work read, *Forked* and *Behind the Kitchen Door* by Saru Jayaraman. Jayaraman is also a compelling and eloquent speaker on the matter. She also heads up an organization called the Restaurant Opportunities Center (ROC). I urge everyone to search out her and watch her speeches. In particular, watch a lecture she gave in Berkeley California titled, "Before You Eat Out...Learning About America's Lowest Wage Earners, July 22, 2018," available on YouTube.

Like many irritating things, tipping seems to have come from the European aristocracy.

According to the book *Tipping*, the practice originated in aristocratic European households. It was a sum of money given to servants. For a long time, a chief complaint of Americans traveling in Europe was that tipping was so rampant. So much frustration, controversy, and violence surrounded the practice that laws were passed to restrict it. Europe decided that tipping was more trouble than it was worth.

So then how did it come Stateside?

There's much debate on this. But it seems primarily fueled by a combination of freed slaves, increased immigration, and prohibition.

In the beginning, US employers didn't have to pay tipped employees at all. The tip was the totality of the wage. After the end of the US Civil War, former slaves started entering the workforce. That's when this practice first seems to have taken root. For some "strange" reason, this new economy was comfortable having blacks work for free.

At almost the same time, here in the last half of the 19th century, there was also a massive influx of immigration. Considering that a violent immigrant takeover founded the US, it's no surprise old immigrants were afraid of new immigrants.

The near-simultaneous influx of immigrants and former slaves meant Americans grew comfortable with the tipping system. Poverty and institutionalized racism also meant most immigrants and former slaves were uneducated. In that environment tipped positions were the most accessible. These same groups also had very little political power.

The general attitude was, "Fuck 'em."

Those with Caucasian backgrounds eventually blended in. Sons and daughters migrated up and out of those tipped positions. Those with a darker complexion tended to remain in the service field. If you need me to explain why I recommend you start with *Between the World and Me* by N'Tahasi Coates.

Then the first half of the 20th century brought prohibition. Restaurants started losing money. "They'll eat you poor, and drink you rich," is an old restaurant adage meaning alcohol is where restaurants make their money. Another restaurants adage is, "The most expensive ingredient in any kitchen is the guy cutting the carrots." Encouraging tipping was an opportunity for restaurants with shrinking profit margins to save on labor.

Civil rights expand. Prohibition ends. The American economy marches forward. Eventually, a minimum wage is established for tipped employees. This wage varies from state to state, but since 1991 this federal minimum wage has been $2.13.

This gets us to the present. Now the American economy is transforming from a manufacturing economy to a service economy. Restaurants are areas of tremendous corporate wealth and economic influence. Through groups like the "National Restaurant Association" corporate restaurants fight to keep the system in place.

Or maybe (as some have told me) this is all activist bullshit.

Marc S. Mentzer wrote a paper, *The Payment of Gratuities by Customers in the United States: An Historical Analysis*. His work implies that tipping came out of, and is directly tied to United States hotel culture. I question a lot of the findings in this paper, but I'd be remiss if I didn't let you know that there are opposing points of view.

In truth, I don't know precisely why tipping has such a hold on the US economy when it hasn't flourished in the rest of the world. I will say that given what I now know, the whole thing makes me pretty uncomfortable.

The Uncomfortable Facts

I'd written 22 pages on tipping before I realized I was only scratching the surface. I decided to reduce my understanding of various surveys, charts, and papers to three overarching truths. These are the practical basics that anyone entering the restaurant industry should know.

1. **The most significant contributing factor to how people tip is whether they like you.** Like it or not, if you want good tips, be likable. It's vague advice that frankly doesn't do you much good. The biggest hitch here is that if you are waiting on a person who holds a racial bias against you or says something like, "You should smile more!" there's a good chance that much of this is beyond your control. Racism, sexism, and various prejudices are the prime negative factors affecting your tip.

2. **Almost to a fault, people tip the way the tip.** If someone usually tips 10%, there isn't much an individual server can do to sway that percentage. Same goes for the 25% tipper, and everything between. If they are happy (for any reason), you will get what they perceive to be a good tip. If they are upset (for any reason), you will get what they recognize to be a bad tip. The role of luck is far more significant than you realize and as great as you are, you are not that special.

3. **The best way to make money from tips is to work at a more expensive restaurant while upping your check average.** If you value your time (and you should), you need to be working at the most expensive restaurant you can. Once there, you should only sell the most expensive stuff.

Boom. These are the three secrets to making money in restaurants.

Offhand I can think of a bunch of anecdotal exceptions to these rules. I also know that given the thousands of people I've waited on, most of the time these rules seem to hold. It doesn't make it better, but these "facts" are the reason why it's helpful not to care about individual tips. There is too much that lies beyond your control.

Let's talk about what you do have control over.

How to Be Likable

End the patriarchy and stop white supremacy. I know it seems hard, but it would help everyone (even most white patriarchs) in the long run. Do everything to remove bias and prejudice from our society. It's easier to be likable in a genuinely fair and equitable society.

This seems like a big, long term goal, but that doesn't make it any less important.

In the short term, people like what makes them happy. One of the quirks of the human animal is that we think we're independent creatures in control of our consciousness. The reality is that we're always partly controlled by autonomous chemical reactions.

There are four chemicals responsible for us feeling happy. Collectively known as "DOSE": Dopamine, Oxytocin, Serotonin, and Endorphins, it's our job to manipulate them.

(For the record. I am not a doctor or scientist, and my opinions here are based on my monkey level of understanding. If you're curious about any of this, talk to a real medical professional.)

Eating a pleasurable meal triggers the release of dopamine and serotonin. Your customer's dopamine levels are primarily dictated by things you have little control over. Healthy sleep, pleasurable music, exercise, and sunlight exposure all contribute to dopamine levels. Depending on the restaurant you might be able to provide excellent music and a sunny room. What you have the most control over is the food you recommend. For dopamine, the general rule is high protein, low saturated fat, and a healthy dose of probiotics. Think bulgogi beef with marinated tofu and kimchi.

Serotonin too has many instigators. The body synthesizes this from a chemical in food that you probably already know: tryptophan. Although often associated with turkey, tryptophan has a significant presence in most poultry (DINOSAURS!). It's also in things like oats, dairy, seeds, chickpeas, buckwheat, peanuts, and chocolate. So push that buckwheat chocolate cake with vanilla ice cream and peanut brittle.

Endorphins are trickier because they are the body's stress response. You get a flood of the stuff with things like fear, and pain. Want a real high from endorphins? Have your customers give birth while running a marathon. Seems impractical. Another thing that helps trigger this is a healthy dose of spice (chilis in everything please).

The takeaway here is that you're going to be feeding your guests anyway, so steer them towards the good stuff.

Let's talk about oxytocin for a minute. Oxytocin is released if we're involved in positive actions. More incredible it's released if we *witness* positive actions. This is our ace in the hole. It's that little something extra we can harness. This means customers get an oxytocin boost if they feel like you're doing a good job and if you're enjoying yourself. If you work in a pleasant environment with people you like while doing your job well, customers will notice.

Lesson? Giving a shit will get you better tips.

If you want better shifts, a promotion, or if you want to work at a more expensive restaurant - this is how you get there. Giving a shit is win-win-win.

Other Tricks

Yes, there are all sorts of "tricks" that have been floating around for years. The issue is that there is no real proof that any of it works. When it comes to crunching the numbers on tipping, one of the leaders is Michael Lynn of Cornell University. In his 36 page paper titled, *Are Published Techniques for Increasing Service-Gratuities/Tips Effective?* he does a deep dive into these tricks, and questions the validity of all of it.

The following list and citations are all taken directly from this paper.

- Use makeup. (for waitresses) *(Gueguen and Jacob, 2011; Jacob et al., 2009),*
- Make their hair blond. (for waitresses) *(Gueguen, 2012; Jiang and Galm, 2014)*
- Wear something unusual in their hair. (for waitresses) *(Jacob, Gueguen and Delfosse, 2012; Stillman and Hensley, 1980)*
- Wear red shirts or lipstick. (for waitresses) *(Gueguen & Jacob, 2012, 2014)*
- Introduce themselves by name. *(Garrity and Degelman, 1990)*
- Use customers' names. *(Adams and Pettijohn, 2016; Seiter, Givens and Weger, 2016; Seiter and Weger, 2013)*
- Squat next to or sit down at the table. *(Davis, et al., 1998; Leodoro and Lynn, 2007; Lynn and Mynier, 1993)*
- Stand physically close to customers. *(Jacob and Guguen, 2012)*
- Touch customers. *(Crusco and Wetzel, 1984; Gueguen and Jacob, 2005; Hornik, 1992; Hubbard et al., 2003; Lynn, Le, and Sherwyn, 1993)*
- Smile. *(Tidd and Lockard, 1978)*
- Compliment customers. *(Seiter, 2007; Seiter and Dutson,*

2007; Seiter and Weger, 2010)
- Mimic customers' verbal behavior. *(vanBaaren, et. al., 2003; Jacob and Gueguen, 2013)*
- Entertain guests with puzzles or jokes. *(Gueguen, 2002; Rind and Strohmetz, 2001b)*
- Forecast good weather to customers. *(Rind, 1996)*
- Write various messages or draw multiple pictures on the check. *(Gueguen and Logeherel, 2000; Jacob et al., 2013; Rind and Bordia, 1995, 1996; Seiter and Gass, 2005)*
- Use tip trays with credit card logos on them. *(McCall and Belmont, 1996)*
- Give customers free candies. *(Strohmetz, et al., 2002).*

You might recognize some, or all, of these tricks. Some of them seem less like tricks, and more like extensions of established facts. For example: putting on makeup and a smile? To quote C.A. Pinkham (@EyePatchGuy) on *Thrillist*:

> *"Attractive women servers make more in tips, on average, than less attractive ones. It's not the way it should be, but humans are irredeemable dickhats, so here we are."*

My recommendation is not to focus on the tricks. Instead, focus on the big picture stuff, and the rest will fall into place.

So get out there and end the patriarchy and stop white supremacy.

Still worried about people liking you?

Don't be.

In September of 2018 the journal Psychological Science released a study that stated: "That following interactions, people systematically underestimated how much their conversation partners liked them and enjoyed their company." In other words, they like you more than you think they do.

If you are looking for something concrete, something I've come across in a lot of dating advice is that people look at the thing they like when they laugh. Tell a joke and watch their eyes. Of course, if you can't tell a joke and they're dating their dining companion, maybe you still won't know.

Since you can't know what's in someone else's head, it's best to get control of what is in yours.

EXERCISE:

Read more, and debate the facts with people in the industry. The real thing you should look into is whether or not tips should rule this industry. In so many ways it seems to hurt more people than it helps. It also appears to perpetuate sexism, racism, and otherwise crummy behavior.

It pains me to say this, but Michael Lynn might be right when he wrote in the paper below that servers are, "overpaid." The current tipping system isn't a good system. It hurts more people than it helps. But if we abandon tipping, it seems servers will absolutely make less money.

But maybe only servers at the top? Is that good or bad?

I have benefited from this system, but it also limits me. I like serving, but it's not what I want to do for the rest of my life. If I take any other job in a restaurant (manager, cook, etc.) it means a pay cut. Can I afford that?

This is a sticky, thorny, value judgment.

In the words of Levar Burton, "But you don't have to take my word for it."

BOOKS:

- *Forked: A New Standard for American Dining* By Saru Jayaraman

- *Behind the Kitchen Door* By Saru Jayaraman
- *Tipping* by Kerry Seawell

PAPERS:

- "Should U.S. Restaurants Abandon Tipping? A Review Of The Issues And Evidence" By Michael Lynn
- "The Liking Gap in Conversations: Do People Like Us More Than We Think?" September 5, 2018, Psychological Science, Erica J. Boothby, Gus Cooney, Gillian M. Sandstrom, Margaret S. Clark
- "Restaurant Opportunities Centers United, Ending Jim Crow in America's Restaurants: Racial and Gender Occupational Segregation in the Restaurant Industry" (New York, NY: ROC United, 2015).

ARTICLES:

- "7 Things You Believe About Restaurant Servers That Are Totally Wrong" November 17, 2017, *Thrillist*, C.A. Pinkham (@EyePatchGuy)
- "What Happens When You Abolish Tipping" August 14, 2013, *Slate*, Jay Porter
- "Tipping Is an Abomination: Here's how to get rid of it." July 19, 2013, *Slate*, Brian Palmer (@PalmerBrian)
- "The Case Against Tipping in America," *Eater*, Vince Dixon (@Vince_Dixon_)
- "Danny Meyer's Servers Claim They're Paid Less After No Tipping, Report Says," *Eater*, Serena Dai (@ssdai)

HOW TO FUCKING COPE

Everything was clean because everything was hidden under a thick winter blanket. It was both dark and bright with the street lights magnified off the snow. Sitting behind the wheel of my girlfriend's car, I faced the bodega across the street. It was shatteringly cold, and I couldn't stop sobbing. My muscles hurt from shaking, and my lungs burned from breathing.

I don't remember if I was coming or going.

At the time I was working at a great restaurant. I wasn't always great at my job, but I was giving it everything I had. I was reliable and loyal, and generally proud of my work.

I'd also become a shadow. I didn't see much daylight, and I didn't spend time with friends. I didn't have relationships with my coworkers. My boss always seemed irritated by my presence. Given my state of mind, that's not hard to understand. My finances and home life were a mess, and no matter how hard I worked I couldn't catch up.

I couldn't afford to take time off to see a doctor. I should have. I didn't know it yet, but amongst other medical issues, I was suffering from sleep apnea. It's marked by fatigue, headaches, difficulty concentrating, memory loss, and irritability. I had it all. These issues made me worse at my job and worse in my relationship. It was a destructive cycle, and I was spinning out.

At the risk of sounding over-dramatic, death seemed like the viable, practical, sensible, solution. I'd finally be able to sleep. I wouldn't have to worry about fighting with people. I wouldn't have to justify my presence. I wouldn't have the constant and overwhelming sadness. I look back, and the healthy options were simple. I needed to take the day off and see a doctor. I needed to walk away from the relationship and the job.

But in my compromised state, those didn't seem like viable options.

At this point in my life, I didn't do drugs or drink. All the sadness was deep inside. I'd cry whenever I had a moment of reflection. It was as natural as drinking a glass of water.

Sometimes I'd obsess about January 3rd of 2003. That's the day I stood beside a 23-year-old man as he decided to end his life.

It was the start of the evening rush hour, and the train was delayed. I was headed into my bartending job. Like this man, I stood at the very end of the platform along with a couple of construction workers.

One construction worker turned to the guy and asked, "Man, when is this train coming?!"

He responded, "Yeah. I've been waiting for this train my entire life."

We all laughed. The train came. He planted his feet, lept off the platform... and that was it.

As we waited to talk to the police, the construction worker shook his head and said, "There were kids on the platform." Recalling that event, I only knew I wanted to do something quiet and private. Sleeping, without the waking.

So, that morning, in that icebox of a car, I picked up my phone and called a suicide hotline.

It was a recorded message. It told me I needed to call back during regular business hours, (you know, when I couldn't use my phone). I even tried to leave a message, but the mailbox was full.

The absurdity of it all led me to laugh uncontrollably. My lungs stung in the cold. I jagged between laughing and crying until I was exhausted. I sat there, completely numb until I gathered myself up enough to get on with my day.

I stayed at that job for more than another year. It wasn't pretty. I had a couple of minor car accidents along the way. When I did see doctors, it turned out that I'd done additional damage to my health. Eventually, the relationship ended, and so did the job.

I look back on it now, and I only needed to pause and look at what was happening. In the world of waiting tables, we talk about always knowing what's going on in the room. In this instance, I'd lost focus on my room.

As RuPaul says, "If you can't love yourself, how in the hell you going to love anyone else."

Now, I have a checklist.

In BOH culture, everyone, every shift, makes a checklist. The checklist is the easy way to keep track of what must get done. Get everything done and you win the day. If you want to be a great server, you need to be self-aware, and you need to know how to cope.

I used to save each dirty, blue-taped, receipt-paper list as proof of my accomplishments. Now I do the same thing with my whole life.

Here's how to build a checklist.

MAKE TIME WITH FRIENDS

According to Vox's Brian Resnick;

"A 2015 meta-review of 70 studies showed that loneliness increases the risk of your chance of dying by 26 percent. (Compare that to depression and anxiety, which is associated with a comparable 21 percent increase in mortality.)... 'Social isolation is far and away the strongest social risk factor out there,' [says] Steve Cole, a genetics researcher at the University of California Los Angeles."

At my lowest point, I was working as a baker, work known for breeding loneliness. But loneliness is not an uncommon problem for restaurant workers in general. No matter the job, restaurant work tends to make people unavailable for regular social events. You'll most likely be working during family dinners, on weekends, and through the holidays.

Given this, many people in the business maintain an excess of industry friendships. It stands to reason that people attracted to the job would have other things in common, but it's not a monolith. Find your people. If you're working at 4 AM or midnight, it's important to find people you like at that hour of the day.

It's also important to know who your friends are. It may not be the people you drink with. Friends help you decompress and let go of the nonsense. These are the people you can be yourself with. We'll talk about emotional labor in a bit. But keep in mind, friends are the people who don't need you to be happy to have a good time with you.

Having an outside community is also essential. Build those non-industry friendships into your schedule. Set up regular dinners on your night off, or take night classes with the straits (I turned to tango and improv).

I'm terrible at keeping in touch with people. I've done lots to try to change that including setting a regular calendar reminder to catch up with friends. At one point I bought a bunch of old, unusual postcards and had people pick out a card and write down their addresses. I could then pull from the stack and drop them a line.

Try to touch base with someone every day. Early on I worked in a kitchen where you had to acknowledge and say hello to everyone as you came into work. This "task" contributed to a feeling of camaraderie and togetherness. Ever since then I've tried to make it a habit.

Better yet, if all else fails, volunteer. It was at my low point that I wound up in a program where I helped teach kids how to cook. It may be one of the top reasons I'm still here today.

Recognizing the people in your life and community helps with the whole empathy thing. And remember, empathy is one of the secrets to exceptional service.

RECOGNIZE YOUR INTIMATE RELATIONSHIPS

Make sure your significant other understands the nature of the business. Include them when you can. One restaurant I worked at reserved the bar on Valentine's day for the staff member's partners. That shift everyone working (FOH & BOH) had five minutes at the bar with their person. Restaurants that understand the importance of the other people in your life are worth working for.

Many date within the business. It can be challenging to work with a significant other. I've done it twice. The first time we kept it mostly a secret. She wanted to move up to management. Sometimes that kind of romantic dynamic can stop advancement. Especially for women. It's shitty and sexist, and it's a reality.

In other words, down with the patriarchy.

In the second instance, the power dynamic was different. We were both servers. But I was old and seasoned, and she was new to the business. From my point of view, she had more to learn. From her point of view, I was a total dick. Maybe she was right. There came the point where leaving our disputes at the door became difficult.

I didn't have a good solution in this case. She grew to hate the restaurant as a whole and quit.

Sometimes working with your person means watching them flirt with other people. That can be too much for some. But, given that serving has an income system based on likeability it happens a lot.

I have seen some healthy relationships develop and grow in restaurants. Often it develops between two people who meet at one restaurant and then go on to work at separate places — thinking of quitting? Take a look around. Maybe it's time to find "the one."

Whatever happens, you have to be with a person you can talk to openly and honestly about work. But, have boundaries. If every conversation is work-related, see a movie... just don't go out to eat.

KEEP TRACK OF YOUR STRESS DREAMS

Common themes: You're the only one in the restaurant. The ticket machine keeps printing. Your feet can't move. You can't find menus. You're getting all the orders wrong. I don't know anyone who has worked in the restaurant industry for any length of time who hasn't had these dreams. Most of us trade them at pre-shift like baseball cards.

Then there are the times when you sit bolt upright in bed and yell, "TABLE 27 WANTED RANCH!"

I was looking for the perfect place to mention the Alie Ward (@alieward) podcast *Ologies* - and this is as good a time as any. Three relevant episodes spring to mind.

First, let's backtrack. In the "Natural History Museum of LA" episode, Ward recommends volunteering when life has you down. Her choise was to volunteer at the Natural History Museum. As someone who also volunteered, I couldn't agree more.

Second, in the "Fearology" episode we meet Mary Poffenroth (@MaryPoffenroth). Poffenroth talked about how what we often label as "stress" is really the human fear response. Listening to her, I realized that in restaurants, both customers and employees are in a constant state of fear. Almost every aspect of a restaurant triggers the human fear responses. Instead of restaurants, we should call them "Fear Cauldrons." Best yet, Poffenroth offers a path to confronting the issue. Listen to this episode to find out about what "RIA" means.

Then, in the "Somnology" episode, Dr. W. Chris Winter (@Sport-SleepDoc) details how shift work (work outside a 9-5 schedule) can wreck you. To quote host Ward:

> *"The World Health Organization does classify shift work as a carcinogen... The stats say that women whose work involves night shifts have a 48% increased risk of developing breast cancer. Prostate cancer is also elevated, along with a host of other cancers."*

In short, restaurant work by its nature is not a healthy lifestyle. Listen to *Ologies*. It may make you realize that this is not the career path for you. Or it might make you better prepared to live the life.

Back to dreams.

If you're holding on to a great deal of fear and anxiety, sleep will allow your brain to evacuate its bowels. Stress dreams are the diarrhea of the soul. Recording these dreams as part of your checklist will enable you to be more accountable. If you're having a lot of them, it might be a signal of chronic stress.

I may never lose these dreams, but they ebb away significantly when I'm working in a good restaurant.

Stress dreams are also often the first signs of the tolls of emotional labor. Emotional labor is a common affliction for anyone who pressures themselves to conform to exterior norms. Emotional labor is a big part of service jobs at any level (nurses deal with this a lot). It's also something a lot of "tough people" don't take seriously. It seems like something you should be able to get over.

It's a real thing, and if you're a member of a minority, you're probably already dealing with it. If you're also in the service industry, god help you.

CHECK YOUR SURFACE ACTING

Emotional labor in the service industry is primarily "Surface Acting." This is the cognitive resource needed to appear happy, engaged, and patient when inside you're screaming.

In "The Hidden Toll of Emotional Labor" from *Psychology Today*, Sarah Rose Cavanagh Ph.D. (@SaRoseCav), says:

> *"Turns out, hiding your true emotions is sort of exhausting. To surface act, your brain uses up resources like attention and working memory (sort of like a computer's RAM), and these resources are limited.... researcher Daniel Beal of Virginia Tech set out to discover whether people in the service industry experienced fatigue due to surface acting... Sixty-four restaurant servers in seven different U.S. restaurants reported on their emotions, their acting, and their fatigue across a total of 2,051 different moments... The results revealed that yes in-*

deed, surface acting is exhausting. Moreover, people who were more emotionally reactive... found it more exhausting."

Want to see how emotional labor affects emotionally reactive people? Find your restaurant's "Don."

Every restaurant I've worked in has a "Don." These people are intense, professional, and capable. Some of them are even tasked with training new servers. They seem great at their jobs, and to some extent, they are. They can be very professional. But, take away societal guardrails, and a switch flips. They become nasty, angry, and sometimes even violent.

Every Don I've worked with could be both very fun and very difficult to work with. Most of them had significant coping mechanisms. The eponymous Don, spent a lot of time in the handicap bathroom doing lines of coke.

Recognize that you are, in fact, doing heavy lifting during your shift. Make sure you have time to put down the weights. This is why you need friends who allow you to let go of the need to perform.

One way that many choose to turn off their mind is through drinking and drug use. Before we address that, let's look at some other, healthier, ways to deal with this chronic stress.

TAKE FIVE TO MEDITATE

I still have trouble with this one. It took me a long time to discover that this was a real thing. For forever I thought this was something people suggested when they didn't know what to do.

Traditional meditation is about letting go of the conscious mind. The goal is to embrace "doing nothing" which is hard for people to wrap their minds around. But, the meat of it is about disengaging from emotional labor and surface acting. Meditation embraces that.

One common outlet for restaurant workers is the cigarette break. It's a shitty crutch. But, indirectly, cigarettes led me to meditation. For years, smoking was my excuse to get off the floor and do nothing but breathe. After a decade I quit the cigarettes, but the meditation part remained. The deep breathing ritual was a critical component.

After cigarettes, I tried other avenues to relax. Massages weren't very enjoyable, but I love traditional Japanese baths. I even gave sensory deprivation tanks a shot. I like "Floating" more than massage and it feels similar to the bath, but for me, deprivation tanks are mostly wet and expensive naps.

A regular, simple, stretching routine was my most effective outlet. It became something to do while watching the news, or listening to a podcast. Time passed, and I replaced the noise with silence and turned my focus to letting go. I now look ahead to my day; I plan my actions. I mentally wander and then get to the end of what I can plan (sometimes it takes a while). Then I step off.

All this leads me to the primary goal of meditation: letting go.

Once, while traveling, I received a last minute invite to a concert headlined by Aqua. If you don't know, they're the Danish band responsible for the song "Barbie Girl." I didn't know their other music, but I figured, "Why not?" On the way there, I smoked a joint.

I got very, very, high.

As we approached the crowd, I found myself half paralyzed. As the crowd sang along and danced with abandon, I lost track of my friends. Giant waves of paranoia kicked in.

I didn't know the city, the venue, or any of the songs. I was in an ocean of strangers in a strange place. At that moment, dancing felt akin to performing surgery. I started to panic. But I knew that if I lost my shit because I didn't know the words to the song "Bumble Bees" I'd tank this fun moment for everyone.

I watched the stage, kept my eyes on the prize, and forced myself to dance. Folks around me even started to dance with me. Everyone seemed to have a good time. Even though I was melting like an ice cream cone on the inside, somehow I managed to have a good time too.

What does this have to do with anything?

Sooner or later you'll have a shift where you feel like you're way too high at an Aqua concert.

You'll go into a shift in a terrible mood, you'll forget to put in an order, and you'll feel adrift. A customer will yell at you, insult you, or grab your arm. A busser might lose a valuable credit slip. The chef will lose her shit in your face.

Life isn't always fair, and that goes double in restaurants.

The most valuable advice I can give anyone working in a restaurant is to let things go. You have to learn to let go of it at the moment. It's not easy, but meditation can help.

One thing that I know helps many of my coworkers is yoga. Primarily divorced from religious practice in the west, some people still get squidgy about that part. I don't do it regularly, but I've found some good stuff in yogic practice over the years. Yoga has always felt like an excellent way to use the body to let go of the mind.

Raised Catholic myself, there's also always good, honest, corn-fed prayer. It's not for me. But neither is natto. On the other hand, I have recently got into shrooms thanks to Michael Pollan and the book *How to Change Your Mind*.

There are so many options.

Find the meditation that allows you to let go, even if it's just watching Marie Kondo on repeat.

GET EXERCISE

There are a lot of runners in restaurants. I myself have participated in three marathons. I also know more than a few gym rats. Adult kickball and pick-up basketball games also abound.

This is a physical job, so working on the physics of your body makes sense.

The most fun I ever had was taking tango classes. Dance is a great way to learn how to know when and where your body is at. This can be anything from strip aerobics to the waltz or gymnastics.

GO TO A DOCTOR

Take advantage of healthcare. There have been so many times in my career where healthcare was not an option. When you have the opportunity, jump on it. Your body is as much a tool of your job as a wine key or bar tray. Take care of it.

Also, considering the mental abuse that comes with the job, take advantage of therapy. You can't tell your bartender everything, and your friends are tired of hearing about your co-dependency.

SAVE MONEY

One of the biggest causes of my past dissatisfaction has been that I felt trapped. Either I didn't have enough money to leave, or the cost of a move was prohibitive. When you save money, save for the far future and, if you can, have something stashed away for flash floods.

I've seen this happen a lot. Even with insurance, healthcare costs are debilitating. Given enough time there will be unexpected moments that take you off your feet. Preparing for everything is impossible. Yet, even having enough money to take a shift off to rest a pulled muscle can be make-or-break. Some restaurants now offer sick-leave, but that still a new phenomenon. Like it or not, I've seen a few restaurants penalize employees for using it.

Emergency Closures. Some restaurants close for short periods because of acts of god. Snowstorms, snapped fan belts, backed-up grease traps, gas leaks, blackouts, and frozen pipes can all shut a place down for a spell. Then there are the restaurants that go under fast and hard. If I had a dime for every restaurant I'd seen suddenly close without the staff's knowledge I'd be Bezos rich.

I recommend looking at every restaurant job, even the great ones, as temporary. Put the money aside now. No matter how much you're sure of the restaurant's stability, there are things beyond everyone's control.

Also, you never know when you might have to leave. If you're thinking of putting in your notice, be aware that some managers will forgo your two weeks. Depending on the manager's sensibilities, they may decide it's not worth having an uninvested employee come in for the next two weeks.

Even using apps like Mint and investing through services like Simple, can be a big help. Danny Meyer's hospitality hedge fund has performed well against the national average. Invest in your future, and know that it comes fast.

It's later than you think.

JOIN A UNION (IF YOU CAN) / GET INVOLVED WITH R.O.C.

In America, Unions are primarily on the decline. As service employees, there isn't much available. Not that there aren't service unions, but few are attached to restaurants. If you're looking for protection of your hours and your dollars, consider a hotel restaurant.

Then there's the organization Restaurant Opportunities Center (ROC), headed by Saru Jayaraman, Fekkak Mamdouh, and Sekou Siby. ROC advocates on behalf of better FOH and BOH wages. They also operate a training center in New York City. As I write this, it seems like this group is making strides. I've never met or worked with a ROC member, and if I'm honest, it's been hard for me to get a hold of people at the organization. But, as it stands, they are still the leading service workers rights organization.

I sincerely enjoy Jayaraman's work and talks, and I only hope to see more both from both her and ROC in the future.

CHECK YOUR DRUG AND ALCOHOL LEVEL

At my first restaurant, I worked with two guys: Paul and Dave.

Paul was in his late 30s, but he could have been in his early 50s with a mop of grey-white hair. Everyone thought he was odd, quirky, and a great server.

Dave was in his early 20s, a hotdog bartender. Everyone loved him. He was the boy next door crossed with John Wayne.

Paul was crazy smart and could do complicated math in his head. He also knew all the moves to the "Thriller" video. He attended Georgetown on a full scholarship but washed out after turning his numerical talents to underground poker games. Eventually, he fell into restaurants. With a burnt-out hippy vibe, he was oddly good with kids. The server equivalent of Occam's razor, he always knew the shortest route between two points. He always seemed to get twice as much done in half the time.

"Do you like boys or girls?" was the first question Dave ever asked me. I wasn't sure if he was fucking with me. He might have been testing my ability to process a question while working, or maybe he was interested in a "bear" like me. I was brand new, and Dave was the gold standard. A fit, young, southern guy with curly blond hair. A pocket-sized Matthew McConaughey. He taught me how to mix a martini correctly and about the value of details. When he wasn't bartending, he was a short order cook at a busy downtown Boston breakfast joint. He even modeled on occasion. He loved his motorcycle and his fiance.

Paul was an alcoholic. Dave was addicted to heroin.

Paul was the first to drop. He had a much longer history of abuse. In the '90s his claim to fame had been his own "brand" of cocaine packaged in National Geographic covers. Back then, Boston was a town where you couldn't buy alcohol in stores on Sunday. That's when he'd come into the bar and purchase an entire bag full of liquor packaged in the kids' sippy cups. Not legal, but everyone looked the other way. He wouldn't stop shaking until he'd drunk at least a handle of booze each day. He "needed" it. A whippet during a party eventually stopped his heart. He was pronounced dead on the way to the hospital.

I did not realize that Dave had a problem. We'd drunk together, and he seemed capable of holding his own. Then one night he came into the bar unable to speak or hold himself up. A few nights later an anonymous caller rang the restaurant. The voice let us know that Dave had OD'd and was lying in the back seat of his car next door.

Paul was resuscitated. He survived. He entered rehab and came back to the restaurant. Over the years he used his number skills to sock away a tidy nest-egg, and he left the business behind.

After the OD, Dave was in a coma for a few days. He woke up and entered rehab. He came back to work for a while, but he wasn't the same. Eventually, his relationship fell apart, and his mother got seriously ill. Unable to cope with reality he took his own life.

As I wrote this I looked up Paul on Facebook, he doesn't post much, but he seems like he's doing okay.

I found out about Dave years later. I'd moved away, and came back for a visit. I met up with some friends for drinks. Midway through the night, his suicide came up in casual conversation. Shocked and drunk and I was in tears while sitting on a rock outside a tourist bar in downtown.

These were some of my first encounters with substance abuse and death in the restaurant industry.

They were not the last.

I have enjoyed my share of excess over the years, and I managed to make it out okay. I've come to the point where I'm happy to say no to drugs, but it could have easily gone the other way.

Many friends have gone through the NA and AA pipelines. Sometimes it works, and sometimes it doesn't. Most of my bartending friends have one month a year where they go dry. Most of them can make it through the month. Some can't.

If in the quiet moments, you desperately want another bump or another drink, or if you're sitting in the front seat of your car with no one to talk to... drop me a line:

f.cking.restaurants@gmail.com

I'm not a professional. I can't solve your problems. But I'm happy to try and listen. (It's the least I can do if you're reading this book.)

EXERCISES:

- **Read.** If you haven't guessed I like to read. I believe that one thing that has helped me over the years is the knowledge that I'm not alone. Books like *Waiter Rant*, *Service Included*, and of course, *Kitchen Confidential* all showed me that misery needs company.

- **Watch *Office Space* and *Waiting* (again).** Admittedly these movies do not necessarily age well. While they've lost some relevance, they are good snapshots of a certain time in the service industry. In particular, the character of "Naomi" in *Waiting* reminds me of "Don."

- **Watch *Chefs Speak Out*.** *The Wall Street Journal* also put out a video: "Chefs Speak Out on Mental Health in the Restaurant Industry: Chefs and restaurateurs talk about the harsh work culture and stigma of mental illness in their industry." It shows that even the people at the top suffer. You are never, ever, as alone as you feel.

- **Watch "Yoga For The Service Industry: Yoga With Adriene"** Adriene Mishler is YouTube's yoga teacher. To quote her: "This yoga practice is designed with the Service Industry in mind inviting relief and restore to the muscles and joints. This is a great yoga sequence for anyone who is on their feet a lot and a great option if you are a caretaker and need to fill your own cup and rejuvenate. Find relief in the feet, the legs, the hips and the back. Nurture a tired neck, shoulders. Take time for yourself. Counteract tension in the body with TLC. Breathe and enjoy!"

- **Volunteer.** I suggest this a lot. Good things come out of giving the most of yourself. Soup kitchens are great, as is any sort of community kitchen. If you can help with Young Storytellers (youngstorytellers.com) that's a hell of a lot of fun too. But maybe mental health is your thing. Check out HealthyPlace.com. From their site, "How to Become a Suicide Hotline Volunteer:"

"Suicide hotlines are looking for qualified volunteers and these qualifications range from experience and education in a mental health field to simply having the right kind of personality to handle emergencies. Keep in mind that even if you

decide being a suicide hotline operator isn't for you, there are typically many other volunteers needed at a suicide hotline that you may be qualified for. Examples of these positions include: Event volunteers, Administration volunteers, Workshop facilitators, Crisis center volunteers."

- **Test Yourself.** Check out the Am I Alcoholic Self Test at the National Council on Alcoholism and Drug Dependence (ncadd.com)

- **Write to me.** Again, I'm happy to listen, or direct you to people who can. You can drop me a line at the following: f.cking.restaurants@gmail.com

THE FUCKING FUTURE

> *"I think that more and more and more really talented restaura-*
> *teurs and chefs from the fine dining world are going to try their*
> *hand at fine casual. They're going to say, 'Why not us?'"*

> - DANNY MEYER, TEDX MANHATTAN, MARCH 20, 2015

Being a great server means learning a diverse array of skills. Master them, and you'll be able to work in higher-end restaurants. Or, you can take the management route, go corporate, and make your millions working your way up that ladder. Your future in restaurants is potentially limitless. It's all about how many fucks you give. Caring enough to always be listening and being willing to learn is your most valuable tool.

Of course, once you give a fuck, you need to think about what the fuck comes next.

What is working in a restaurant going to look like in a year? Five? In a decade or less, large parts of the business will likely, drastically, change. But, as we've discussed, usually the best way to get things done in the future is to have a plan now.

There are many potential changes. But what you do will depend on your direction, so let's look at your options. Let's start with your immediate future.

You Want to Move Up

There's nothing wrong with wanting to be a server and to stay a server. I know people who have built happy lives around the flexibility and versatility of this job. It's what makes them the most money with the most flexibility. At the end of the day, if you can live a happy life, you have a leg up on most everyone. Your happiness should always be your first goal.

At the same time, it is not unnatural to expect that you might want to move up.

A big part of giving a fuck is showing up and being present. This means listening, and demonstrating that you're listening through your actions. Most restaurants worth working in will recognize who gives a fuck. It's these fuckers who have the highest potential to move up.

The first step here is that you have to tell management in no uncertain terms that you want to move up. Whatever you do, even if they tell you point blank, "You are an amazing server," do not assume a promotion will come. There are a million and one reasons why they may not offer you advancement. Let's start with the simple fact that they probably need good servers.

Some places will ask, "Have you considered management?" That was how I wound up in my first management position. But, if it's something you want, don't wait for the offer.

At the same time, be aware that they may say no. If they do, don't get defensive. Some restaurants don't want to hire from the inside. They may have flimsy reasons for this, but if they don't want you, you probably don't want them either. If you can keep a cool head and ask questions, they may offer you legitimate information to help you improve. Remember: no matter how good you get, you're never perfect. Be receptive to guidance, regardless of whether it's positive or negative.

It becomes much harder if they give you an unclear answer, or if they skirt the conversation. In management, there is a general attitude that it's better to avoid a difficult conversation rather than risk alienating an employee. This is not to say that that's always what's happening. Some managers are simply wearing too many hats and are easily distracted.

But if you're tired of not getting direct information, I'd take this as an indicator that they like you as an employee, but don't consider you management material. This might help you decide to pursue a management position somewhere else.

Like in any relationship, if you can't communicate and if you want different things, it's probably time to break up.

Once you've decided that you're interested in management, prepare for the transition. At a basic level, this means knowing that you might need to save some money. There is an excellent chance that in a management position you will make less money and have to work more hours. If you have a partner or a family, prepare the people in your life for the transition. Going from being a server to a manager is a career shift that I've seen kill relationships. It puts significant strain on the two big relationship killers: time and money.

While a manager uses many of the server's skills (empathy), they use them in different ways. A manager is the last line of defense between an angry person and a happy person. But unlike a server, they have to manage that line between customers, employees, chefs, and owners simultaneously. Inevitably someone gets short shrift, and being able to mitigate the "loser's" disappointment is a big part of the job.

But, there's more. Remember the most stressed, panicked, drowning, weeded, moment you ever had at work? A good manager is a person who helps you out of that hole. A great manager helps you do it yourself. A manager doesn't do the server's job, but they do create the environment for the server to do their job better.

As a manager, your priorities will shift. You have to make choices that benefit the whole restaurant. A server's job is to look at things up close. A manager needs to build a staff that communicates the small things, so that they can then connect it all to a larger picture.

Read up on things like food and labor costs. Learn about your kitchen equipment. Hone your management skills. Above it all, your most valuable skills will be to learn how to teach and lead people. Part of that is listening, and part of that is being able to correct someone without demoralizing them. If you haven't yet read, *Setting the Table* — now is the time. Be able to have a coffee with someone and discuss "Hospitality Quotient."

Prepare yourself to be in a lot of positions where you think you know more than you do. This can be a humbling job. Deal with it. A manager has to be able to trust their team, but also show them new paths.

But you know all this already.

I got a piece of advice from a friend and restaurant manager several times over. Trendy chef-driven restaurants seem great, but the best place to get your first management job is a corporate chain. Why? Proper training.

Most small restaurants, even great ones, don't usually hire managers until they're understaffed. As a result, when a new manager comes up the restaurant is unable to take the time to teach. It's a steep learning curve and only the prepared survive.

But when you hop on board a big chain, they take the time to cultivate. A well-trained manager is a guard on their larger investment. Corporate chains also pay a hell of a lot better.

But if you don't want to be in management, what then?. Maybe you'd rather maximize your paycheck, and instead of moving up, you'd rather move on.

Moving To Another Restaurant

The biggest secret of restaurants: no matter how different any two restaurants seem, they are, eerily, identical. The nuts and bolts of the job stay the same. The reality is that most differences are cosmetic and semantic. Much is a matter of style. It makes sense to work in a place that reflects your style.

Finding the right restaurant culture for you can be a bit of a trial and error thing. There have been restaurants I've liked a lot, that weren't the right fit for me. It's like dating. Some restaurants are one-night-stands. Some are long term relationships. I've also had restaurant divorces and once I became a restaurant widower. If you're lucky, you find the one you marry.

At the end of the day you always need to think about one thing: Do you dread going to work? How happy or sad would you be if you never had to walk through the doors again?

But, your time is also valuable. Under the tipping system, a restaurant that charges more for their food, means you make more for your time. Sometimes a more expensive restaurant may seem like it's out of your range of experience. It's probably not. A fancy restaurant is mostly just a cheap restaurant in a better suit.

Find the place that makes you happy, and keep an eye on it. If you can, get to know the staff. Watch the job boards. When the opportunity presents itself, present yourself. Be careful though. There are restaurants I applied at that I no longer feel comfortable frequenting because of poor interviews.

Bagelsaurus: I will always miss your bialys.

Once you decide to leave there are a few ways to handle your departure. Some people will no-call/no-show. That's not cool.

Even in a large city, the restaurant business is smaller than you might realize. People talk. The Ghost of Ghosting will follow you.

Be prepared. If you give two weeks notice (or more), they may take you off the schedule right away. This action may sound unfair, but this is the two-edged sword of leaving. It's best to think of this as an, "It's not you...," situation. An employee on the way out can be a liability. The restaurant wants to trust you, but they know they shouldn't.

When a person quits, they are not as invested as they once were. Since the server is the forward face of the restaurant, some managers don't want to take the risk of having someone who is checked-out in that position. A manager's job is to put the needs of the restaurant first. It can be easier to be short staffed rather than deal with someone who doesn't give a shit.

Speaking of management, that can also be a reason to leave. Managing at the same restaurant where you've waited tables can be awkward. Moving to another restaurant may be what helps you advance.

Moving to Another Industry

Many chain restaurants offer ways to transfer within the company. Mobility can help a lot if you're looking to make a more significant change in life. After college, I wanted to move to a bigger city with more opportunities. My job at the Cheesecake Factory gave me the chance to move across the country, and land in a strange town with a job already in place.

Twice in my life, I've left the restaurant business to pursue other careers. This isn't always a smooth transition.

There was no bigger shock for me than transitioning into a 9-5. Lunch breaks, paid sick leave, vacation time, and a 401K -- it almost didn't seem like it could be a real job. The funny thing is that the higher up I went, the people around me seemed to have fewer practical skills. In the end, I moved up because I learned how to manage people, an ability that came directly from restaurants.

Something I hear from a lot is that "everyone should wait tables at least once in their life." I do not agree. Some smart and capable people are not cut out for the job. That said: many healthcare professionals might benefit from waiting tables. In the reverse, I've watched more than a few intelligent restaurant people move into the medical field. Want a version of this job that offers respect, better advancement opportunities, and higher income? The answer is medicine.

The quickest step away from the restaurant business is sales. There are jobs selling liquor, wine, beer, soda, and food. If you feel a corporate future is what you're looking for there is industry goliath Sysco. They sell everything.

There are many options when it comes to selling wholesale food, and not every opportunity involves losing your soul. There are farm co-ops, foragers, oyster farms, apiary collectives, dairy farmers, and more. Outside of comestibles, once I was offered a job selling BMWs. I've worked with restaurant folks who've sold everything from used cars, to drugs, to Tiffany Jewelry.

I've also worked with a million and one actors. At least one server became well known for playing a cook on TV. There have also been writers -- and at least one government policy wonk (no, not THAT one).

All these other jobs have something in common with serving. They all need people who excel at persuasion, empathy — and the appearance of giving a shit.

But maybe what you really want is to be a Chef? You're not in a bad spot, but you're going to need to prove your worth, because most Chefs are sick and tired of shitty servers. Run food like a god. Talk to the cooks. Buy them beers. Understand just how good you have it compared to many of them.

When it comes to the Back of House crew, I've met many former photographers, printmakers, and bookbinders. All these fields are detail oriented and require a certain level of meticulousness. They also necessitate developing a gut level sense of aesthetics.

If you're going to hang with them, pay attention.

Now that we've talked about your future options let's talk about the future of the industry as a whole.

No More Cash

When I started in the business, you could still smoke in most restaurants. At the end of the night, I walked with cash because debit cards still didn't exist in the United States. Less than half of people paid with credit cards and traveler's checks were still a thing. Cash is now about as rare as public smoking. There are a few outposts: podunk towns and small businesses that still operate on the all-cash model. This is rapidly coming to an end.

There is a statistic I've seen pop up repeatedly that claims most servers underreport their income. An unintended side effect of the disappearance of cash is that tips can be recorded more accurately.

Some wage accountability is essential. It allows us to accurately understand how things like race, age, gender, and more affect income. We need this. As long as the "underreported income" argument is out there, legitimate and necessary discussions are being undercut.

Of course, with more money in this "imaginary" state, there is the increasing issue of wage theft. According to a March 12, 2018 editorial from *The New York Times*; "The Department of Labor's wage and hour division estimated that nearly 84 percent of full-service restaurants it investigated between 2010 and 2012 had violated labor standards, including but not limited to tip violations."

Accurate accounting may only cut out *some* of the graft associated with the business.

There's more to this though.

Recently some states have started to ban restaurants that *don't* accept cash. It's a stickier issue than you might imagine. For more on this read Melissa McCart's (@MelissaMcCart) article "The Problem With Cashless Restaurants" (Feb 15, 2018) on *Eater*.

No More Tips

Once we have a more accurate idea of what people are making, losing the tip standard may be the next big step. Many are trying to move toward this model with Danny Meyer at the forefront. Many who have dipped their toes into this stream have already abandoned the attempt. Even Meyer admits to having some trouble with this system, but he's still plugging forward.

I talked about this at length in the chapter about tips. The main stumbling block comes from one thing. Options. If a server makes more at a tipping restaurant than a wage-only restaurant, what is the incentive to stay at a wage-only shop?

That's still being worked out.

Part of me would look forward to the elimination of tips, especially if it can improve the work environment. But there's also a big part of me that'd miss the risk and reward of an unreasonable payday.

Something that may play a big part in the future, and what may eventually lead towards transitioning away from tipping is education. As more people become educated in the system, more people will find it inhospitable, and spending habits dictate a lot.

The other day I overheard someone complaining about a "3%" fee tacked on their bill for the kitchen workers. "The problem," he said, "is that I don't understand why the restaurant can't just pay their workers. Why do I have to do it? The servers I understand. They get a reduced wage."

There's a lot to unpack in that statement.

It's important that people within the industry talk about the tipping system, both with their coworkers and also with the general public. Can you defend your paycheck to the line cook who makes less in 60 hours than a server does in 30?

The Mechanics of Operation

When I started bartending, I once got a dressing down for using a jigger on a drink. It was from Duncan, a regular who used to read pop fiction and hit on the waitresses at the service bar while getting blasted on Stingers (brandy and creme de menthe). According to him, and my fellow bartenders at the time, the general expectation was that only rank amateurs would use a jigger.

These days I have a hard time imagining frequenting a bar that didn't use a jigger. It allows for consistency and quality. I expect a higher quality beverage from any bar that jiggers their drinks.

Unless I'm looking to get wasted, that's when I want an irresponsibly sloppy freepour.

As we move into the future, we are looking at an increased level of automation and precision. I used to work with a guy I'll call "Angry Chef." AC would decry the use of sous vide and other "molecular" techniques. He talked about how real skill meant that you could do it all on your own.

Especially at the advent of the technology, I don't doubt that it was misused, but the more that cooks become familiar with it, the more they'll use it in better ways. I can imagine there must be ways to use sous-vide systems to increase quality and save money all while increasing output.

I mean, I trust robots to make almost every car I ride in. There may come the point where I'd expect the same from my food.

Food is software. Chefs are programmers, and cooks are kind of like... punch cards. I doubt it'll be universal, but some restaurants will outsource menial labor to technology that doesn't get hungover or stabby. Restaurants already rely on running with the smallest staff possible. This is only more of a standard that has already been established.

I can hear AC now, telling me to, "Eat a bag of dicks."

Like it or not, there is a higher level of quality when a smart Chef has more control. What distinguishes a Chef from a cook is not necessarily cooking ability. Instead, a great Chef can teach and inspire random people to cook at the crazy high standards of their imagination. Imagine if you could download your vision and skip the middleman. If anything the tech explosion may lead to a decrease in cooks, and an increase in Chefs.

Add to it all, a decade long (plus) cook shortage. How can line cooks afford to live in a place like San Francisco? We're heading towards a future where urban areas will only be able to afford food costs provided by "non-traditional employees."

As cities sprawl, restaurants that do new and exciting things will continue to appear further and further outside of urban centers. Only celebrity chefs can take risks with expensive overhead - but why would they? People will go out of the way for a high profile chef. It makes sense for almost every new restaurant to go out where the rent is cheap. Places like Minnesota.

FOH and BOH are both at risk. The increase in delivery orders affects FOH as does the push by high profile restaurateurs towards casual dining.

Look up places like Eatsa, Spyce, and Creator. These are three restaurants that have started to figure out ways to cut out both the cook and the server. Just as porn delivery drives the tech industry, fast food drives the restaurant business.

It's hard to imagine McDonald's isn't looking for ways to pioneer a restaurant without employees. Once McDonald's has gone full Skynet they'll partner with the self-driving fleet Uber is developing. Within a decade, not a single human soul will be necessary to get a Big Mac anywhere with access to a road.

This is Trump's moonshot dream.

Eating In

A fact that gets bandied about a lot is that after years on the rise, Americans now spend more on restaurants than in grocery stores. Then someone pointed out that this was because restaurants were becoming more expensive. I've been told that the spending change actually reflects the reduced costs of eating at home.

Blue Apron, Hello Fresh, Plated. At first, these were all named as threats to restaurants. But even they have started to drop off. As I write this, Blue Apron's stock has aggressively shit the bed. It seems that people realize that if they have time to cook, they usually have time to shop.

In the last year, there's also been the advent of things like LaPiat, which is a "food sharing app." Think of it as an Uber for home cooked meals. Currently only available in Toronto, it allows people to sell off food that they make at home to anyone using the app.

I don't know what any of this means.

Maybe it will continue to fragment the industry?

Perhaps it means more and more "delivery only" restaurants that operate out of a central kitchen and deliver to homes but have no storefront.

Or, perhaps the Amazon drone army will take same day drop-ship meal kits direct to your door from Whole Foods. Maybe restaurants and supermarkets will continue to merge and become central food hubs. Imagine giant Cheesecake Factories where you can buy pizza, tacos, and dim sum. Then maybe you can order tableside delivery of chocolate sauce and toilet paper for the house.

Maybe the future of food belongs to the person who can curate the best snack-box subscriptions. That's kind of like being a waiter, but you'd do it from home.

But maybe the server job will merge with more traditional managerial positions. Then you'll have a person whose job is to coordinate a robot food army while smiling and scrawling a "Thank You!" on the receipt. The human touch. Someone has to stay on board the self-driving food truck as it does its deliveries. Who else will keep it clean, stocked, and bring the bags of food from the automated cooking system to the front door?

Chefs as "Bands"

After the tools and language arguments were debunked, the ability to create art was touted as what separated humans from animals. Then I listened to "The Beauty Puzzle" from *Radiolab*. So... nevermind. It's official, we're all animals.

All of us that is, except for the robots.

Robots have the potential to excel in every human skill. But you can still say that what separates man from our Cylon overlords is an ability to create art. So, let's build on that.

A long time ago I had this discussion with friends that restaurants are conceptual. My argument was that it comes down to the parable of the ax. "I bought this ax 40 years ago, I've only replaced the handle twice, and the head once — is it still the same ax?"

Given enough time, a restaurant can change locations, menus, and the entire staff. Then what makes a restaurant? I'd argue that a restaurant is a feeling. What else equates to the incarnation of a "feeling"? A song.

If a dish is like a song, what if you thought of the Chef as a singer/songwriter? For most of my life, this is how bands operated: they'd produce an album, and then tour in support of the album. What if a restaurant concept was the album, and then the team behind it went on tour to promote it?

Imagine a chef, or a group of chefs, conceived of a menu. Maybe they're all about celebrating a particular cuisine, or a specific food philosophy. They then assembled a menu and wrote and published a cookbook for that menu. Then they'd go around promoting their book while doing pop-ups (live shows). They would function as a band on tour, doing media events on the way, etc. A true moveable feast.

At the end of the tour, maybe it generates enough excitement to becomes a brick and mortar location. Or maybe, they write another "album" and keep touring.

Hospitality wonks love to use this often misattributed quote, "They may forget what you said, but they will never forget how you made them feel."

Food and music are the fastest ways I know of to recreate a feeling. Given that this quote is attributed to at least six different people, it seems eerily accurate.

Coupled with the rise of the "experience economy," a celebrity chef with a "restaurant" that can travel is a valuable commodity. Chefs who build a following could set up anywhere with a fan base.

Look at Las Vegas. In an odd reverse, you could say that it's where bands go to set up brick and mortar stores. I mean Lady GaGa has a "residency" at the MGM. It's also a gourmet food oasis located in the middle of nowhere. If you can't book a trip to Spain, France, and England -- fly cheap to Vegas and sample food from Andrés, Robuchon, and Ramsay.

All I'm saying is that if you can eat Nobu sushi in the desert, you should be able to enjoy an inspired tasting menu from the same chef in both Omaha and Des Monies.

More Casual

If Danny Meyer says it, it's probably true. I've heard about the expansion of casual dining for years. It makes sense. Big numbers offer big rewards. Bigger numbers offer bigger rewards. A few upscale restaurants are great, but Danny Meyer also has Shake Shack. The Shack has 162 locations and had an IPO in 2015. David Chang is also branching out into fried chicken joints, dessert shops, and at least one convenience store.

If it is about the quality of the food, who cares if you get the world's best dinner from a paper-lined plastic tray? This feeds into everything else we've already talked about. Delivery. Convenience. Lower labor costs.

Casual dining is the blue jeans of food. Pair it with a ratty shirt to clean the house, or dress it up in a sports jacket for a night out.

The Third Revenue Channel

The "third revenue channel" is extra revenue streams. This includes, but isn't exclusive to, things like delivery and take-out.

It can also be cookbooks, shirts, hats, and even offering an unused dining room as a rentable "meeting space." These are all things related to the restaurant but don't involve eating on premises.

Years ago Starbucks talked about turning their coffee shops into a "third place:" a space other than work or home where you spend your time. Both these terms reach for a similar idea. It's a thought that has thrived in dense population areas like Hong Kong, Tokyo, and Paris. How do you grab people's attention (and money) when space is at such a premium?

There are many new ways that people are trying to shuffle together food and commerce. At the German chain Ziferblat instead of a standard bill, you pay a per minute fee. That fee grants you access to a basic kitchen, and a "free" pastry spread similar to a motel breakfast bar. Its primary goal is as a workspace, offering room rentals and AV services.

In many ways, restaurants might trend back to their origin as secondary draws. Restaurants started as a place to get "restoratives," usually soups, and usually located in a hotel.

It was food that offered a feeling of hospitality while paying for another service. But in 1765 Monsieur A. Boulanger sued for the right to serve his food separate and apart from a hotel. From this first schism, we get everything from Panera to Per Se.

One concept we never lost, but that has drifted in quality, is the idea that food makes "retail therapy" even more attractive.

Department store restaurants are an old and familiar concept. One only needs to visit a Cracker Barrel, IKEA, or get Pizza Hut from a Target to see that this is still a thriving model. The food isn't always the main draw, but it's there to get you to circulate in the store. Movie theaters and even banks are now promoting themselves as restaurants and coffee shops.

Many of these ideas have not been well integrated. Often the food isn't that good, or the atmosphere is lacking. In these situations, the restaurant is a secondary, thoughtless, drive.

But what if you could get the world's best croissant from your loan officer?

Restaurants will endure, but how they work will be constantly changing.

Figure out which waves you want to ride, and hop on.

❋ ❋ ❋

EXERCISES:

- **Find a six-year-old.** Ask them how they would make a restaurant in the future. Play fake restaurant. It may not teach you much about what is to come for restaurants, but working with children always offers some fantastic insights. And, at least you'll get in good with your boss ten years from now.

- **Pay attention to "real" future restaurants**. Watch *Idiocracy, Blade Runner, Demolition Man, Sleeper, Cloud Atlas, The Fifth Element, Star Trek, Red Dwarf*, and *The Hitchhiker's Guide to the Galaxy*. Or, for a view of a semi-futuristic alternate timeline restaurant check out the Steve Martin movie *L.A. Story* — (L'idiot).

- **Get high or drunk and discuss restaurants of the future with your friends**. Drunk and high not your thing? Eat until you are explosively full. Then, try and think about a.) what you need to feel better, and b.) what would get you to eat more...

- **Watch a YouTube video.** "David Chang on What's Wrong with Delivery Food" (TechFest) *The New Yorker*, Oct 14, 2016

- **Write up a business plan for your ideal restaurant.** I can't teach you how to do that, but maybe you'll hit upon something! Consider employing me. After writing this book, I'll need a job.

EPILOGUE

This was a book about empathy. If you skipped to the end, I'd ask you to remember one thing: The secret to being a great restaurant worker is universal empathy.

Ta-da.

Pretty much every moment that I was working on this book I doubted its relevancy, or that I actually had anything to say.

Many of you reading this may now be saying, "Wow, you powered through with this pile of flaming garbage, huh? Well, I guess that means I should write my book then!"

You should. Write that book.

I need to thank all of my first readers and idea bouncers; Meghan, Liz, Ann, Alex, Vik, Jen, Jenny, Emily, and Amber. In particular, I need to thank Kelly and Pat who basically made this entire book possible with their generous hospitality, and willingness to let me drone on and on about nutty things that no one outside the restaurant industry gives a flying fuck about.

Also, thank you Willis & Mexi. For the last three years I'm sure I've been a pain in your butts, probably wondering why I don't seem to take a lot of my own advice. All the same I've appreciated both your patience and the paychecks.

A very special thank you to all of the Chef's who've let me profit off their work, but especially Chef Drew. It's always wonderful to work with someone you can get comfortably heated with and still be friends. Drew, ring the bell when you need hands for your own place. I'll happily run food.

Special thanks to Erik for letting me blow him off to write this sentence.

Lastly, here's to the Toronto Public Library, and the Cambridge, Massachusetts YMCA for providing the space and WiFi to make this book possible.

If you have any interest in learning more about my further writings, you can find me on Quora (J.S. Kohout), Twitter (@RestaurantJunky), and Instagram (@restaurantjunkie).

Better yet, if you find a glaring error in this book, drop me a line at the following address, and I will try to fix it for the next edition: f.cking.restaurants@gmail.com

Well, I hope you enjoyed at least some of this.

See you out on the floor.

[1] "7 Restaurant Scheduling Stats of 2017," The 7Shifts Blog. By Chris de Jong (Director of Marketing at 7shifts)
[2] Clopen-double: Working the closeing shift the night before, and then opening the next morning into a double shift.
[3] Sidenote: it's easier to sell a drink when people are alone. In a group (especially at lunch) there is an element of judgment that occurs. People look to their dining companion for permission, even if they want to get a drink. Even if their companion couldn't give two shits, people feel on display, so they shy away.
[4] Working at the Cheesecake Factory is not a bad job *at all.*
[5] An important thing to realize that just as cooks get bored of cooking the same dishes day after day, managers occasionally feel ennui towards their staff. It's nothing personal, but dealing with the exact same problems from the same people day after day can be a bit grinding. Keep this in mind when your manager seems to be "absent." Learn how to have empathy for your manager. Learn their likes and dislikes, and learn how to "manage" them.

www.ingramcontent.com/pod-product-compliance
Lightning Source LLC
Chambersburg PA
CBHW021818170526
45157CB00007B/2628